The genius of Fr. Giussa[...] to speak directly to the h[...] [...] mystery of God—stands out clearly in his encounters with other searchers. This particular encounter sets before us a number of human realities and gives each of them an extraordinarily dramatic depth and urgency: birth, death, freedom, memory, pain, redemption, sacrifice, and hope.

—D.C. Schindler
Author of *The Politics of the Real*

For Giussani and Testori, the stakes could not be higher: either we as a culture will begin to recall where we came from and thus rediscover the meaning of our lives, or we will turn our faces and walk away from the source of all love. Toward the end of this brief but powerful little book, I found myself moved to tears.

—Paula Huston
Author of *The Hermits of Big Sur*

Two men sit down to carry on a discussion of the meaning of hope in the context of birth and what it means...and the result is a white-fiery explosion of theological and psychological insight. The truth is: I was blown away by this exchange.

—Paul Mariani
Author of *Ordinary Time*

Perhaps now more than ever before we need this profound, prophetic book which shows us how to deal with the "forgetfulness of being loved" in the light of the "catalytic encounter with a human presence" made possible in the Incarnation of Jesus Christ.

—Fr. Peter John Cameron, O.P.
Founding editor-in-chief of *Magnificat*

THE MEANING OF BIRTH

LUIGI GIUSSANI
GIOVANNI TESTORI

THE MEANING
OF BIRTH

foreword by
Rowan Williams

introduction by
Giuseppe Frangi

translated by
Matthew Henry

SL/.NT
BOOKS

THE MEANING OF BIRTH

Slant Books
P.O. Box 60295
Seattle, WA 98160

www.slantbooks.com

HARDCOVER ISBN: 978-1-63982-106-8
PAPERBACK ISBN: 978-1-63982-105-1
EBOOK ISBN: 978-1-63982-107-5

Cataloguing-in-Publication data:

Names: Giussani, Luigi; Testori, Giovanni.

Title: The Meaning of Birth. / Luigi Giussani and Giovanni
        Testori.

Description: Seattle, WA: Slant Books, 2021.

Identifiers: ISBN 978-1-63982-106-8 (hardcover) | ISBN 978-1-
        63982-105-1 (paperback) | ISBN 978-1-63982-107-5 (ebook)

Subjects: LCSH: Giussani, Luigi. | Testori, Giovanni. | Giussani,
        Luigi -- Interviews. | Birth (Philosophy)

FOREWORD

WHAT DOES IT MEAN to recognize yourself—or any other being—as a person? It's a question that comes up in all sorts of different contexts, from debates about the unborn child to animal rights to issues in the development of artificial intelligence, and the answers are chaotically diverse. But in this book we have an answer that is genuinely startling and distinctive, with the broadest implications. We are not invited to think about what morally or intellectually interesting qualities something needs in order to count as a person; instead, we are reminded of a bare physical fact: we were born.

There was a moment when our parents underwent a transitory visitation of self-abandonment and a new material process began, a clustering of cells into a new organic unit. And this cell cluster, as soon as it begins to exist as a definite organic reality, is launched on a process that will inevitably involve a unique relationship to the rest of the physical world—a story, a destiny, a set of memories and hopes, a way of speaking and seeing.

Life was begun *for* us, not *by* us. It was given us, in the shape of this cell cluster; a literal physical place was made for us, and this is why and how we are persons. We grasp the reality of our personal nature by acknowledging that we have been given life, that we are always *someone's child*. If we are blessed, that recognition remains a point of reference for us: we know we are loved, that at the beginning of life there was a moment where human self-abandonment allowed God's own act to weave itself into the world's fabric in a wholly fresh way. If we are in any way deprived of that recognition—if our parenting has been indifferent, abusive, repressive, rejecting, if we know that conception itself was marked by cruelty or violence—we are injured at the very root of our being.

But the woundedness of so much of our contemporary culture is less about these extreme and tragic individual injuries and more about the way we are encouraged to forget what it is to acknowledge our dependence, the basic level at which we are receivers of life from elsewhere. We feed ourselves endless fictions about the self-sufficiency we think we long for, we are ashamed of having to receive and depend; we give value and respect to lives that deny this receiving and depending, and dismiss lives that are especially, visibly, dependent—the unborn, the very young and very old, those living with disabilities and limiting conditions. We can't embrace the truth of our own birth, it seems, and we resent those who can—those who have never forgotten that they are children—while at the same time feeling a deep and painful nostalgia for that central conviction that we are *given* life at the hands, ultimately, of a love which simply desires that we exist.

It is this conviction that makes it possible for us not to hate ourselves. If we embrace the truth of our birth, we embrace the fact of our material, organic being—and we embrace the organic physicality of the other, wherever that other's face is shown to us. My recognition of my own birth is inseparable from the recognition of yours;

what we most deeply have in common is not an abstraction called human nature but the common fact of this material moment of beginning-to-be—being projected into a story and a calling, a set of unimaginably extravagant possibilities. Lose sight of this, and the face of the other begins to blur and recede, just as my own sense of my value and solidity blurs and recedes. I and the other alike become abstract, defined not by the gift of birth but by all those lesser and more localized identities which set us apart from each other.

Abstraction is the enemy repeatedly hauled out into the light of day in the conversation that we are privileged to overhear in this book. We are forcefully reminded that one of the undeniable trends of capitalist and militarist modernity is the disappearance of human faces. You can fight a war without ever seeing the face of your opponent (and this was before the development of drone warfare); you can spend years in the employment of a business without ever seeing the face of an employer or a client (and this was before the development of online retail, electronic banking, zero hours contracts). We can imagine a global catastrophe that is "nobody's fault" because power has drained away from identifiable human agents into the hands of vastly complex mechanisms and algorithms (these days, the catastrophe of an environmental devastation driven by financial modeling which tells us that it is beyond challenge or change, no less than the risk of global warfare unleashed by impersonal calculations).

As many biblical scholars have said, the "principalities and powers" of the New Testament are for us today the faceless influences that steadily strip away our decisions from us. Resistance is all the harder because they are so intangible; at least in the dreadful totalitarianisms of the twentieth century, there was a certain visibility to evil and coercion. How do we learn to resist when we do not even know where the levers are being pulled?

All that our two eloquent dialogists say is if anything more pertinent now than when their conversation took place. The forces of abstraction are stronger, the pressures to deny or forget our dependence are shrill and insistent; and the result is a pervasive feverishness of self-definition and self-protection, struggling to cope with the terrible burden of creating and sustaining who we are by our own resources.

The Psalmist says to God (in the old Anglican translation): "Thou hast set my feet in a large room." Proclaiming the Gospel of Christ today requires of us as never before not only a clarity about the largeness of the room (that alone can lead to a sense of paralyzing disorientation) but a clarity about the one who "sets our feet" there, who gives us a place to be which we don't have to earn or justify. If that liberating recognition can pervade our hearts and minds, the ethic of justice, solidarity, compassion, mutual delight and reverence becomes the obvious way of living humanly—living as if we had been born, as if we had been desired, invited, loved.

As it is beautifully put in these pages, this is an ethic of Christmas: the mystery of God's own self coming to birth among us so that we may at last see and love the dependence we fear or deny and acknowledge in one another the mystery we must look upon with wonder and thanksgiving.

—Rowan Williams

INTRODUCTION

FEBRUARY, 1980. In a beautiful country house on the river Ticino, a few kilometers from Milan, Giovanni Testori and Father Luigi Giussani met each other for a conversation that gave birth to a book. They needed a peaceful place where they could put themselves in front of a tape recorder, and this house was truly a welcoming, ideal spot.

Father Luigi Giussani was the founder of Communion and Liberation (CL), a movement that in those years had seen tremendous growth in Italy, particularly among university students. Giovanni Testori, on the other hand, was a writer, an art critic, and editorialist for the Italian daily newspaper, *Corriere della Sera*. They had met two years earlier when an article by Testori on the assassination of the Italian politician Aldo Moro had drawn the attention of some university students from CL, who came to meet him personally and then took him to meet Father Giussani.

The understanding between these two men was immediate, helped along by their shared roots in Lombard Catholicism. Testori, in fact, was a writer who, rather than defining himself as a Catholic, described himself as one who had always reckoned with Catholicism deep down. His personal path, intense and sometimes brutally dramatic, was turned upside down in 1977 after the death of his mother. The newspapers spoke about his "conversion." In reality, Testori's conversion was simply the experience of an encounter: an encounter with those young people about whom he knew nothing and who came knocking on his door. And then, above all, the encounter with Father Giussani: "Giussani was a person who censored absolutely nothing of what I was, not even those parts of me that could have created scandal," Testori would say, referring also to the fact of his homosexuality.

The son of a family of small Lombard manufacturers, Giovanni Testori was born in 1923 in Novate Milanese, a town just outside Milan. He graduated from the Catholic University of Milan with a degree in art history, with a thesis that was in part also censored by the academic authorities because of its openness to the aesthetic of contemporary art. He was "adopted" by Roberto Longhi, the most important art historian of twentieth century Italian art and a leading scholar of Caravaggio. With Longhi, Testori became one of the principal scholars of Lombard art: we owe to him the rediscovery of the Sacri Monti, those extraordinary artistic monuments which were built starting in 1400 at the foot of the Alps. In the meantime, he debuted as a fiction writer, publishing a successful collection of stories set against the background of a post-war and economically booming Milan. From some of these stories, Luchino Visconti made his most famous film: *Rocco and His Brothers*.

The arc of Testori's life was very similar to that of the film director Pier Paolo Pasolini: the same generation, the same attachment to their cities of birth or adoption (Milan and Rome), the same freedom in critiquing every hypocrisy of religion and church. Above all, Pasolini and Testori were considered intellectually heretical by the official Italian intelligentsia, both progressive and conservative. When Pasolini died in 1975, Testori took over as editor of the front page of *Corriere della Sera*: like Pasolini, Testori was an observer who was not ideological, who went against the tide, not only with particular positions, but above all by choosing to put the human factor at the center of every one of his columns. This anti-intellectual approach unleashed furious polemics against Testori, exactly as it did with Pasolini.

It was these pieces published on the first page of *Corriere della Sera* that drew the attention of a group of young people from CL who studied at Catholic University. From that encounter, a new and important experience was born for Testori, one that would also have consequences in the arts. His impassioned engagement with young people was to be centered in the theater. Together with Emanuele Banterle, then a student at Catholic University, and the Company of the Ark, created by a few students from Forli, he staged a production of his text, *Interrogatorio a Maria* (*Interview with Mary*), which had more than 500 productions throughout Italy. In the summer of 1980, it was performed at Castel Gandolfo for Pope John Paul II. Together with Banterle, and with one of the most famous Italian actors, Franco Branciaroli, he founded a theater company, Gli Incamminati (Those En Route), destined over the years to become an important presence in the national theater scene.

At the beginning of 1980, Giovanni Testori asked Father Luigi Giussani to meet for a discussion that could be turned into a book. It was not a simple or obvious idea. Testori, the famous writer, humbly and attentively followed this priest who was not only popular among young people, but always in conversation with the great thinkers of the past. For Father Giussani, "*The Meaning of Birth* signaled in some ways a turning point in the history of CL," as the journalist Lucio Brunelli wrote in his introduction to the reprinting of the book, published as a supplement to the weekly *Il Sabato* in 1982.

In what way was it a turning point? Brunelli explained: "Its newness does not come so much from the judgments that Giussani expresses. Those of us who had the fortune to participate, starting in 1976, in the meetings for the leaders of Communion and Liberation had already heard these things. The newness comes from the fact that for the first time, and without mediation, these ideas became a public fact. It was a break with the schemes that pigeon-holed a certain image of CL." The book, in fact, "made possible by the intellectual courage of Testori," was put out by the principal publisher in Italy, Rizzoli, and so was destined for a much broader public.

This innovative fact detailed by Brunelli shows up in the dialogue itself: *The Meaning of Birth* dismantles an image of CL that was maliciously elaborated by the mainstream media. In other words, the image of a movement of "crusaders," of "fundamentalist troops" who move only in reaction to the attacks of the secular enemy (Brunelli). CL was boxed in by the strategies of the ideological opposition, who depicted it as the advance guard of a Catholicism in search of a new cultural and social hegemony. Instead, Giussani profited from this public occasion to clarify his thought with words that still move us by their precision: "This is the time of the rebirth of personal awareness. It is as if we can no longer make organized crusades or movements. A movement is born with the reawakening of the person."

This quote brings us to a fuller understanding of the book's title. The "birth" to which he refers is the birth of the person. Father Giussani says: "Paradoxically, the little David of a liberated person stands up against the Goliath of the state, which is the powerful instrument of the mechanism that destroys man. For me, this is the sign of the times for Christians.... It is on this fragility, this ultimate weakness of the truth, that the power of God inserts itself with its promise.... This is how the concept of a 'movement' is born...the ideal of a movement, which exists as if it did not have head or tail—we don't know how it happens. In fact, the birth of this movement happens in the most inexperienced and unarmed particle that exists: that is, the person."

Testori himself, in dialogue with Giussani, gives witness to his own personal "birth." At a certain point in the dialogue he reveals that he has lived Christianity like an undesired stain "stamped on my forehead," almost like a mark that he cursed. "You were like a child locked in the basement," explains Giussani—that is, with an interior life that was chained and frightened. "But, in such conditions, no one in the house could sit by calmly," Giussani goes on to underscore. That is, his condition could not be extraneous to us, it could not but trouble our hearts as well. In the dynamic between this question and its answer, Testori relives the moment from two years earlier, when he felt himself welcomed by Giussani and, as those who witnessed it say, he could not keep back his tears. The meaning of birth is not something that we acquire once and for all; it is a question that remains always open, as we entrust ourselves at every moment to the One who loves us.

Giovanni Testori died on 16 March 1993. For years he had followed the life of CL with great passion and freedom. Thanks to their relationship with him, dozens of young people were able to gain clarity and find their own personal path in life. This was a dynamic that Father Giussani remembered, with sorrow, when he celebrated the funeral of Testori in the parish of his hometown, Novate Milanese. "And so you became the father of these young people, who in their confusion and impotence (in Italian, *sperdutezza*, a key word in this book), they found in you a point of reference, just like you found a point of reference in them, a point of hope in them. 'They came!' you said, and you surprised those who heard you. 'They came!' But who? Those glimpses, those moments of hope, for your eyes and your heart; and you threw yourself into relationship with them, and created everything in relationship with them, and so you 'recreated' them. What deep thanks they give you now!" *The Meaning of Birth* is a book that in the true sense of the word has borne fruit in new life.

—Giuseppe Frangi

THE MEANING
OF BIRTH

THE CRIB & THE CROSS

Giovanni Testori: Here we are. You know this encounter should have become its own book—a stand-alone book. Instead it takes on the weight—and also the joy—of launching a collection of books. The first thing to recognize would be that the intention to put this book together has already given us a gift that neither you nor I could have hoped for. Here we are then, setting out on this encounter with the responsibility of setting out, at the same time, on a collection of books that affects us directly. And for this reason, they will be for everyone.

For days I have been thinking that maybe it would be good to start this conversation from a particular. The particular is this: what should we name this collection? For my part, I have been focused on two titles: one could be *Books of Birth* or, with a little more intimate connotation, *Books of the Crib*; the other, which seems better, and that does not exclude the first title, but contains it, is *Books of the Cross*. I have not been able to get these two titles out of my head, these two realities.

I also had a third title in mind, *Books of Hope*, which is within the other two titles, which overlaps and embraces them: that of birth (of the crib) and that of the cross. Maybe I am catching you off guard? But launching a series of books, firmly, decisively—even with all the errors and shortcomings that we bring with us—that also wants to be integral, a collection of Catholic books, what title would you propose? Given the titles I have tried to suggest to you, which would you choose? And why?

Luigi Giussani: I would choose *Books of Hope*, because the word hope catches a primordial expectation and opens our attention, as well as the road to an answer. Now, birth and the cross are already part of that answer; the title that would imply the answer would not be understood immediately, because the one who hears the word, who reads the word, would not necessarily know how to grasp the way in which God, through his action, incarnates it. I would use *Books of Hope*.

GT: About what you have just said, I have a question: why is it that for me, and the greater part of humanity, the physical awareness that is linked to the word birth, to the word crib, and to the word cross, is so much stronger? I ask because for me the manger and the cross—that is, Christ's birth and passion—have a weight, a resonance, a fate that is so strong, so ineliminable that if it were possible the title would be: *From the Crib, through the Cross, to Hope*. And because we can't have a title that is already a book, we will sum it up, as you propose, in *Books of Hope*.

But I wanted to ask you to help me, to tell me why (and I believe you feel this very strongly) not only in me, but in so many—maybe in almost everyone or in the greater part of young people (it is true that I am not young, you and I are the same age, but I am young to certain truths, also to the Truth)—I wanted to ask you why these two moments, that constitute "the moment," have such a great weight: why are we so marked by them?

LG: Because the expectation of human hope in you has already had a great history, and then, I believe, you know its urgency and its powerlessness: therefore the expectation moves toward a cry—a cry for the answer, that which in Christianity we call an *announcement*. The announcement of a fact that, piercing through all our weakness, smallness, and meanness, presents itself as an embrace that remakes us, which means the embrace of a new birth, an embrace that creates a total renewal. In sum, it is a rotten flesh that flourishes, according to the meaning of the words that Jesus said to Nicodemus.

GT: Hope—which is man's destiny, his path—is born, physically, cellularly, from a state of pain and at the same time from a state of happiness, because it is an awareness of the reason for being, but also a pain, precisely the pain of birth that already has within it the pain of the cross. Now every man has his cross, whether he recognizes it or not—small and unworthy compared to the Cross of crosses, but also large, because every man is God's creation, so the cross of every man is large even in its smallness, in its hesitation, in its shame and its betrayal. Man is a great event. Every person is an immensity multiplied to infinity.

At the center of this immensity there is a hope that is born and that is tied to pain. This is the problem: that is, the observation that joy makes one happy, and restores hope, only in the intensity with which we suffer for it, participate in it, incarnate it, understand it, assume it, recognize it—only in the instant when, for all these reasons, it becomes the pain of God. Woe to the one who is afraid of pain, of the pain that comes from birth. Because this would mean prohibiting almost all the development of man toward hope, almost all of the development of man within the design of God and within the blood of Christ to arrive at the One who truly exists, to the time that is no longer time, to the space that is no longer space, in which all our time and all our space can find their eternal, total consecration.

For this reason, I believe that the greatest reality of Christianity is the resurrection of the dead—the cosmos that will be inhabited, not by ideas, not by hypotheses, not by memories, but by bodies risen by participating in charity or by excluding it. I believe that precisely because this resurrection of the dead, this resurrection of the body will happen, because the cosmos will be always inhabited by bodies—that is, by the children of God and by the brothers and sisters of Christ. For this reason I believe that we cannot do without pain, without the cross.

LG: When I spoke about the great story of your hope, I meant to connote this presence of pain. Without the experience of pain, there is no experience of humanity, which means, of an urgency that has been hunted down, embattled, defeated. I also agree with the first point. There are two aspects of this pain. The first, which is carnal, is the pain of those who die of hunger by the thousands in India, Vietnam, the Pacific islands—the carnal pain of hundreds of thousands of people, of millions dead in wars, in concentration camps, or hundreds of thousands who suffer cold in the inhumane conditions of the gulag. Such is that physical and carnal pain that we feel when our friend dies or one of our family members passes away, or in certain moments of sickness, when someone with dark thoughts is invaded by the terror of no longer being able to manage and thinks that it is a serious illness, an incurable illness; this pain that becomes a sharp pain or a dark sadness, that isolates us from everything.

But there is the possibility in the life of so many, especially for us who live in this kind of society (but I think that it is an observation that would apply to other historical times)—there is the possibility of satisfaction, of compensation—I don't know how to say it—of balance in the things of life. We can therefore read the *Corriere della Sera* and be struck by the headline about refugees from Vietnam and then be calm for the whole rest of the day, so that the next day, it is like a surprise when we find the same tragic documents. That is, our kind of society favors a life that is, so to say, generic—as if we were making a great effort to distract ourselves from, to forget, pain.

In order for pain to become what you said about it—a path to a new birth, to a presence—for it to become a birth and an Easter cross, cross and resurrection, the other aspect of pain must occur in man—that is, the pain of our own evil, of our own evil as dignity, therefore of our own evil as compared to ideal images—what Christians call the pain of sin.

There is a tragic alternative when one is struck by carnal pain (in oneself or in others, either way). That is the alternative of a rebellion that denies reality: "this world doesn't make any sense." Or, to put it in other terms: "God does not exist because there is this pain." This does not happen in the pain of sin, for which the blow of carnal pain frees us for the perception of another, more acute pain, of a different nature.

But it is in this moment that the wonderful paradox begins, in which the same carnal pain becomes a door to heaven. It is like when the whole sky is full of clouds and a blue strip starts to come through—that is, a liberation. When the carnal blow, the carnal pain—I don't know how to say it better—becomes a metaphor, becomes a symbol—when it points to, uncovers, the veil of another pain that is moral pain, the pain of sin. There, at that point, only at that point, moral pain begins within carnal pain, and pain becomes liberation.

In a certain sense, carnal pain, becoming a sign, connecting itself strangely, unknowingly, with the pain of its own inadequacy to the ideal, of its own condition of not being obedient to the ideal, of not subjecting itself to the mystery of things, itself becomes liberation. In sum, it is already in itself a liberation from rebellion and therefore from meaninglessness. And it begins to rebuild the truth. Because the problem is not that man should be sinless, but that he should be true—that he should begin to place himself, to locate himself in his point of reality and truth. So it is as if the end of days, it is as if the extreme of things, it is as if the mystery of God begins to turn into a smile toward him, into a regenerating and welcoming attitude toward him. It is as if God begins to make him conquer.

ABANDONMENT & LIBERATION

GT: In my life—before in one way and now in another—I have retraced the road of birth, and it happened to me just like it happened for some of my characters. There is a character, Ambleto (who is a twist on *Hamlet*), whose monologue of "to be or not to be" is replaced by another, very long monologue in which he goes back to find the moment in which his father and his mother embraced each other, loved each other—when he became a little drop, the first moment. When I wrote that text, there was the shadow of a curse on me, but perhaps even in that shadow there was already a hope.

And this is the extraordinary thing. That if you go back behind the pain of birth, you find an act of love: because my mother and father loved each other in God— in Christ they loved each other. It needs to be said. I think that we do not need to be afraid to say it, because these are things that if they are pronounced in hope become sacred in themselves.

Look, there is a moment of abandonment that is lost in love, of abandonment and liberation. Who knows how much pain and trouble were behind and within them before that moment. I don't know if it is right—I will try to say it—then, maybe, we can remove it or correct it. A day off work. My father worked, my mother already had other children; and then there, in that bed, where I was born, which is the same bed where I sleep now, the same bed where they died, where they loved each other, where they united their burdens and their affections, this love of theirs, and they became what is said also in the holy books "one flesh and one soul," and they probably set free their trouble in their love, their pain in their joy. In their great joy and abandonment they experienced a joy that goes beyond what we know, what we understand, what we are familiar with.

LG: The word abandonment is right and adequate, because it is precisely as if we welcome something from beyond in that moment.

GT: This is also a grace of God, because this abandonment happens within the womb of the sacrament.

LG: It is the very abyss of the force that makes everything, that arrives in those moments—those moments that so many times would be totally illogical in respect to what came before.

GT: Instead they acquire a logic, an intelligence and a light, because in that moment God was participating— if I can say this with a word that may be irreverent. No, it seems to me that saying this is inevitable. God participated, entered within them, and brought me to birth. Most of us are born from a moment of total love, from a moment of love that arrived to the point of no longer being able to know itself except with the help, intervention, and presence of God.

LG: Abandonment! It is beautiful, because it is the word that indicates the other power that completes the fact, that brings about the fact, because it is the power of God, the mystery of God.

GT: This is how I was born. This is how I became a son. Then I, and not only I, but everyone, the young people I encounter—with whom I meditate on suffering, so that suffering may no longer be isolating, so that it may not be a fact on which one can even be tempted to complacency, but becomes a liberating fact—believe we have understood that pain should lead to liberation, not once, or maybe once for all time. But when we say once for all time, it means experiencing it again every day, every hour. It should lead to our becoming children of the Father who is God and children of an earthly father who is our father in the flesh.

At that point pain is no longer isolating; it is already a pain that can be shared. And it is precisely here that you feel the real sense of guilt, of disobedience, of the inferiority of your being a son with respect to the grace of having a heavenly father and mother within your earthly father and mother. It is at that point that one feels the pain that becomes liberation—liberation and hope, because it immediately generates in man the awareness of the totality—of the Trinity, of the Father, of the Spirit, and of the Son who generates in man the need to be himself a father—a small, minuscule father, perhaps, but still a father. This is hope, so that we walk toward the eternal as father and son, mother and son. This is the path that the Lord has chosen; there is no other.

Now I feel that this awareness of being a child of God, loved by the Spirit, redeemed by Christ—and of being at the same time the child of my father and mother, a brother to the brothers I have already had and will have later—is the beginning and the proof of everything. Then it happens in the family: I reach out to the brothers of my father, to the sisters of my mother, to the brothers of my mother, to the sisters of my father, to my cousins and then to the whole world, then this sense of being a child, this sense of the gift of being a child becomes like a hymn, a *Gloria*—this redeems pain. You carry everything on your back because you feel your pain, the pain of your historical father, of your historical mother, of your grandfather, of your grandmother, of your brothers who surround you, who will come after you—you carry all of it. But everything is bearable, not because it is diminished, but rather because it has its center in the parallel and contemporaneous fatherhood of God, in the contemporaneous illumination of the Spirit, and in the contemporaneous redemption of Christ. Because it is at that point that suffering becomes awareness of being a child and thus a sign and fruit of love—that the prime mover is love. Then this greater love needs to incarnate itself in new pain: otherwise the awareness of love would be unreal—it would only be a hypothesis.

It often happens to me during the day, but above all in the evening, when I walk through the streets, when I walk by these enormous houses, or even in small towns, but above all in the big cities—anyway, here in Milan— and I see these closed windows, and I think about all the men and women who sleep there: unhappy, happy, healthy, sick. Then I think: in this moment there is someone in those houses who is loved, in this moment God is there to continue his creation, the true meaning of creation. Then I feel this murmur, this rumble, this silent cry of pain. All of a sudden this comes over me.

One time I was struggling. As soon as I noticed this, I said to myself: we are all damned to this immense lake of pain where we experience only injustices, sufferings, inequalities, and depravities. Everything seemed to be channeled toward meaninglessness and death. Now, without the pain lessening at all, without it weighing down on me any less, I had the certainty that everything would be channeled toward hope. It is a kind of silent, terrible glory that I experienced. I don't know if this happens to you.

You hear all these breaths when people are asleep—for example, in the summer when the windows are open. It's not that I want to enter or violate anything that happens in those houses. What I am saying to you comes to me from the breath of those who sleep, possibly of those who suffer, of those who are sick—a breath that would be unbearable and un-nameable if it did not receive its name from this parallel divine and human sonship that brings with it the recognition of other brothers, everyone equal in this parallel sonship, to walk toward a hope that is the only possible true hope—that is, the awareness of this pain carried to its depths, down to ashes and glory.

To come to those who live most intensely the muteness that modern culture has sought to impose on pain (not the true modern culture, which has never silenced pain, although it has given a distorted voice to pain)—to come, then, to the young people, the thing that astonishes me, that humbles and exalts me at the same time, is the indivisibility that they show. This is an indivisibility that did not exist in my generation because we were divided between pain and hope. But today's youth seem able to live the indivisibility between pain and hope—whether those who live oppressed by pain, or those who are raised up by hope. What astonishes me is that in their words and in their lives (because they are words that flow like blood and, thus, are life; for the rest, that indivisibility exists also in their gestures), whether they are lost or instead whether they live to save the world in the redemption of Christ's blood, the pain of hope and the hope of pain are never really separated.

These are indivisible realities in young people today—in fact, even those who are lost from too much pain. But within them they have a tragic, possibly suicidal, awareness that it is no longer able to separate pain and hope. Certainly there is some possibility that was not given to them—maybe it is our fault. We do too little, we pray too little, we believe too little, we feel too little, we incarnate too little this fact of being like children and therefore brothers. But even in young people—as far as I have been able to listen to and experience them—there is that inseparability, even if it is turned in a negative direction. You have been living for decades, Giussani, the story of the young generations. You have seen them pass by—rather, they have passed through you; and you, so young yourself in many ways, you have been a kind of father, a brother.

PAIN & HOPE

LG: Yes, young people, especially the most recent generations, can be defined as the living place—the new place—where pain and hope are identified. In fact, it is as if there was a groan in them—a cry like that of children when something has gone wrong. The groan comes from the physical will—the will that the body has for a tranquility that is born from equilibrium. In this sense, I understand everything you are saying, I understand that this is like a groan. In a banal way, we could say that there is something lacking—that is, a presence that is missing. What is lacking is the presence of what you are calling birth.

GT: It is as if they have not yet been able to affirm that birth in a total way. But this is the profound response young people can offer to the materialistic culture—a culture that has (ironically) become absolutely abstracted from the material, that no longer considers materiality—that uses it, manipulates it, abuses it, employs it, assassinates it, strangles it, kills it.

LG: That takes it only as a pretext—

GT: Because if it respected materiality, it would see that at the bottom of materiality there is birth. So the greatest answer to this materialistic culture—whether of consumerist or Marxist varieties—is what the young people have discovered: the inseparability of pain and hope, for those who kill themselves or those who accept their ruin—or those instead who with difficulty ascend to love and to the realization of hope. They have discovered the inseparability of the act of being children—between the act of birth and the hope of becoming fathers and mothers. This is the answer that no one wants to recognize, but true life is to be found there.

LG: Exactly. I would say that the groan in young people—that your words have helped me recognize in all the faces of young people today—is precisely this absence. It is as if birth were not present and as if they had still not reached the awareness of their dependence, which means the awareness of being loved. The response we make to this unity of pain and hope depends on whether the intuition of their birth emerges, even in a shadowy way, as you say—which means the feeling of being loved. Because the supreme feeling is that of being loved. So their way of reacting depends on whether this intuition breaks through the dense clouds, or not.

GT: Why doesn't this feeling break through? Why did it once allow survival—that is, compromise and ambiguity—and today it no longer does?

LG: Because before there wasn't this absence. That is, this intuition was preserved carnally, through the relationship between parents and children in the nexus of the family. Now, though, the triumph of hope as a kind of mad will, as a human madness (and the events of 1968, from this point of view, are key), has pushed this feeling of being loved far away, this sense of birth in which everything is implied. The possibility of humility is implied there—the possibility of a sense of one's limits, and at the same time the possibility of security, of certainty, and of proceeding in time. In short, security—that which the baby has in the arms of his father and mother—is there. At one time there was not this absence. Now there is this absence of the feeling of birth.

GT: But, paradoxically—and not meaning to defend them, but rather to participate with them deep down in all their disarming and tragic truth—paradoxically, is not the moment when you feel this absence the moment when you can discover the presence with greater force than what comes slowly or passively, so much so that if it were suggested slowly and passively, we would have let it die?

Why, how is it that it died in them? Was it not because we are no longer aware of ourselves, or are only aware of this being loved as an echo? It is not that you suddenly go down to zero. You arrive there by backing down, by degradation. Being loved, the sense that "in His will is our peace," that in accepting, that in gratitude for being children, is contained all our possibility of being children and of being human—if all of this is degraded little by little, it is because we have let ourselves become distanced from the original flash of meaning—that is, from the point that I told you before: the point of birth, of abandonment. Then, in this moment, young people find themselves in front of this absence, which maybe is not an absence, but rather melancholy, a terrible nostalgia. A man does not kill himself from absence; he kills himself from nostalgia.

LG: Nostalgia, this is perfect. Nostalgia is the feeling of an absent good.

GT: Which presupposes, though, an inclination toward the absent good, an inclination that maybe in preceding generations was not there. I do not want to be pro-youth at any cost, but it seems to me that this is the case.

LG: The force of expectant waiting in today's youth is without comparison with respect to that of young people thirty or forty years ago.

GT: Even if they pay dearly for it—or maybe *because* they pay so dearly for it. Because then, this society that has made them unable to perceive the positivity of being loved has only offered them prisons. What should be the liberation of the will of man by being loved has become a total slavery, has become nonsense—the exploited man, the reduced man, the divided man, man as a thing, man as an object, man as a number, man who is manipulated, killed. It is from here, from this new, terrible servitude, that the rebellion comes. And woe to us if we let it fall into the void. It would truly be a genocide, here and everywhere.

LG: Let what fall in the void?

GT: Pain, joy—the pain through which we recognize the nostalgia for the truth that we lack and the painful joy of those who have already had the gift of being able to take this truth in hand again. Or the painful joy of letting ourselves be taken up again by this truth. They are two parallel gestures, two holy gestures. If one who has the duty (and we too are among those who have this duty) does not do everything so that this situation matures toward hope, but instead lets it slide toward inactivity, then this will truly result in genocide.

I remember the interview published in *Il Sabato* with Mother Teresa, when she said: "There is only one Christ here and there, here with you and there, to be carried; there is a mission here as well which is different but equally necessary." In this case, here, in our Western society, this mission has a terrible, grave, extreme responsibility. I believe that if we do not give our whole life for this situation of life, that if we do not give all our awareness of being loved so that this being loved becomes joy—the awareness and will of everyone, above all the youth—then I believe there will truly be a massacre—a massacre of souls and bodies, that can never be separated just as they will not be separated there, in eternal peace.

LG: This is truly the massacre of the innocents perpetrated by those in power—power that ranges from parents to the state. But I return to the image that you brought up about this groan that most of the time goes unexpressed, but that we see expressed in certain faces, which is owing to the lack of affection. It is here where normally parents go wrong in this unfortunate generation (I don't know if our generation was more fortunate, because we are the ones who generated this infamy). The parents of this suffering generation naturally wanted good for their children. And yet....

It is on this point that I wanted to interject before: because we cannot give to a man, we cannot give to a child, the feeling of being loved, we cannot make him understand this, if we do not communicate the joy of a destiny. Then pain changes its aspect—that is, it changes meaning, it changes its sign and becomes a condition for joy. It is the joy of destiny that parents have not communicated to their children.

GT: It is the joy of being themselves children that they have not communicated to their children.

LG: This is where I wanted to arrive: that fathers and mothers have claimed to be fathers and mothers and have not paid attention to the greatest sign—that they themselves are children.

GT: They no longer remember that abandonment—

LG: Exactly! They have never been made aware of their being lost; they have not looked within the abyss that drew them into the very gesture that united them! Which means: they have forgotten. It is as if the gesture that united them and the fruit of generation was theirs, something born of them.

GT: I ask myself if they have not gone farther, having forgotten that they themselves are children—

LG: They have forgotten that they too are children.

GT: And in doing this they have also forgotten that they too are loved.

LG: This is a religious absence, the absence of a father.

GT: This has created, in the very act of their love, a separation—a separation between love and the possible birth of a child. There has been a moment in which something like a sword has intervened—and then the children quickly have a laceration, a cut. Even if in their gestures they have been fathers and mothers, they have broken that unity, that bond.

LG: Which means their children are born as if they are not loved.

GT: Certainly they are born detached. There is a share of emptiness, an immense precipice of emptiness. In fact, in my book *Ambleto*, in that process of which I spoke before, at a certain moment the protagonist says to his mother something like: "In that moment, at least in that moment, did you love each other?" It is a type of non-official orphaning—unregistered as such, but even more terrible.

LG: Yes, this insight is really profound.

ATTEMPTING TO FILL THE VOID

GT: So then young people have to do everything over. They have an enormous burden to fulfill, but also one that is glorious. They must fill that hollow space, that void, that precipice which existed between their father and mother in the moment of their birth. All of this is their duty, their burden, and it is terrible. So I understand if they hesitate, if they lose themselves. I would do anything for them not to lose themselves. But I understand it. I understand much more a young person who loses himself than a mother or father of forty or fifty who continues in their inertia.

These young people have to glue this emptiness together, to put it together with their blood, with their spit and with their flesh, because all of this is truly a matter of flesh, spit, and blood. So I also have a great respect for their eventual failures. I don't want them to fail. I say again that I would do anything for it not to happen to them. But I find them humbly greater than the apparent certainties of those half-parents or casual parents!

Just think: you and I have had the fortune to have a father and mother who loved each other. There was nothing but love between them, and yet it seemed to me like I already had to retrace everything. Think about those young people! So there is only one thing needed.

It is a question of blood—it is there that love becomes charity. The flesh, the spit, and the blood that glues things together, that reconnects them: this sense of being loved cannot happen without effort, travail. But it also cannot happen except through the flesh and blood of the One who holds everything together—of the One who reconnects everything, of the One who has given us hope again, the hope of returning to the Father.

It is for this reason that I wanted to call this collection *Books of the Cross*, because it comes down from there—it is that blood, that out of charity continues to mix itself with the blood of this generation—and it is only that blood, the blood of Christ—that can fill the emptiness opened up by those swords.

LG: You spoke about your father and mother who loved each other their whole lives, who were good Christians, and yet even you had to do this whole process over, to put things together again. It is a process that everyone has to re-do; it is a process that has to happen in everyone, this tiring ascent and descent to find the point where we have been loved.

But the recognition is that we are made by God, that the blood of Christ is truly within the drama of this religious desire that shows up as a visible and unmistakable proof against which we cannot argue—this is why God died for us. We cannot be persuaded that we are loved if we do not come to perceive the work of God and of the mystery of God within the carnal will of man and woman. Without this dimension, without this ultimate opening on the true horizon—that is, the horizon of God—we cannot truly recognize that we are loved. What the Gospel says, from this point of view: *Those who are born not by the will of the flesh, not from the will of man, but from God,* shows that within the clump of cells that has appeared in the flesh from the relationship that generates man, there is the flash of the ideal. This means that the flash of destiny—the availability of man and woman to destiny—appears clearly only here. And it is here that gratitude can become not only pure toward one's own father and mother, but also the beginning of a support—that is, a hint and sign of certainty and thus of hope.

GT: Within this flash the most mysterious thing, the deepest thing, but also the most holy thing, is that this flash of destiny is not something separable from that clump of cells. In my opinion, it is not a light that enters later—it is a light that is already there—a light that loves, determines, and forms that life.

LG: It is the awareness—

GT: —that exists even if you do not believe it exists.

LG: Perfect! But it must play out within the current culture, in the most elemental sense of the term. It must be present and play itself out also unconsciously—it must be received, even if not explicitly, within the normal culture with which man feels himself, sees things. It is this that has been expelled—consciously expelled—with a will. It has been expelled by the will of the "super-man" and thus everything has been reduced, banalized.... How to say it? The blessings of the state are not able to bring to birth the meaning of what is implied, as you said, by the very first clump of our existence.

GT: For which reason I believe that "making believe it does not exist" because we cannot do anything but pretend to forget this original implication—

LG: —but by saying "no, no, no," we can persuade ourselves of it.

GT: Yes, but you are haunted by the truth, because it is there—it enters within you in that moment and stays there forever. And then you experience, first a tragic situation, then the defeat, and, in the defeat, the contradiction. Then the superman has become the opposite of itself: it has become the objectification of man, of man who has tried to forget this flash of destiny, which was not only a spark, but the leaven of that clump, because the truth is precisely this. The first and ultimate truth: it is the very clump of cells which is the will of God. Having forgotten this, man has reduced, instead of enlarged, the clump—he has reduced it to plastic material—he has reduced it to a unit that can been indecently used, blinded, starved, killed, assassinated.

LG: This is what the Gospel says: *I am the cornerstone, whoever accepts me will build on me and whoever does not accept me will have it fall on his head.* It will smash his head: this is what the Gospel says.

GT: And here we have arrived to the head and the body which are imprisoned, to the head and the body which have been smashed. In this pseudo-liberation of man, we have arrived instead at the gallows, at assassination, at genocide.

LG: Yes, in the East and in the West.

GT: Everywhere. Even here, in our country. Earlier you used the word "culture" and it seems to me that as you said it, in that moment, it was pronounced at the level of its essential meaning. We need to take it up again in that sense. At its depth, culture is the continual awareness—then the incarnation, the continued development—of being loved.

LG: Because all evil is born from this lie, by which man tries to define himself in practice or in theory as though he forgot or cancelled the memory of his birth.

GT: I ask myself: is it possible to be an atheist or is it only possible to believe oneself or call oneself an atheist? For me it is only possible to believe yourself or call yourself an atheist, because outside of the Father, in truth, it is not possible to believe or say anything about yourself. To believe anything, to say anything, to make anything of yourself, is only possible in relationship to the Father.

LG: It is only possible to call yourself an atheist, as you correctly said before. We cannot obliterate or cancel this original factor because it is constitutive of our reason. It is what permits our awareness of ourselves and of the world. This perception of our original dependence that is essential to reason, this dependence that, translated into human language, is made true, truly human, should translate itself into the words "being wanted," being made—because we *are* wanted, we *are* made.

It is not possible to eliminate this reality. It is possible, as you say, to act as if it didn't exist. But this acting as if it didn't exist starts from the feeling we have made of ourselves. It starts therefore from the feeling and image that we build of our relationship with others, with things, and therefore is the start of a systematic awareness of reality, beginning from our own "I"—that is, it tends to become a private culture of that reality.

Now this image invests that clay, that energy of contact and attachment that the "I" has with itself and with things that is called will. And as it pertains to the will, so it involves our freedom. Freedom is the need to adhere to one's destiny—destiny as the essence of an attachment to things, of attachment to being, therefore, as an infinite source of affection. When freedom is lost, security becomes a mere simulation—every word is a simulation because it no longer corresponds to what has originally determined and willed it.

GT: A culture that presumes to do without this act of dependence—which is thus an act of growth, an act of glory, an act of glorious humility, because it signifies being truly and consciously within creation—

LG: —it is an act of humility that establishes itself, that affirms itself—

GT: —that establishes you and affirms you in the center of God's will. Therefore, it is an act that makes you grow—and not, as we hear continually, that humiliates you. Rather, it is an act that strengthens you. A culture that diminishes this recognition of being wanted is a culture that is condemned, always, in the effort to forget that it is wanted. And in fact in modern culture the truest expressions are those that sound the alarm—those who have said: "it is not possible; it is not licit; pay attention to where we are going."

The true, great, tragic expressions of our time that can be read as documents of the poetry and history of man are those that have shown that the path the culture was taking was cut off and separated from the beginning and that therefore would also be cut off and separated at the end—that any sort of arrival was in fact impossible. I believe that the true culture of our time has been this, the one that proposed the atrocity, the impossibility, and the absurdity of this situation.

After all, let us reflect: in the moment when man believed himself free from this being loved, in the moment when he no longer wanted to live this act of awareness and of humility and produced the acclaimed well-being and equality (without taking away anything from the merits of those achievements)—in a moment like this, when man seems to have finally obtained his so-called liberty, the culture has done nothing but accuse the result as being full of malaise, blindness, slavery, and death. While man proceeded toward so-called well-being and equality, the true culture has done nothing but accuse the anguish, the inequality, and the impossibility of existing on those terms.

There has been a culture that accompanied this fake progress, but the true culture has criticized it, besieged it, not given it rest—has borne witness, shouting: "Look out, we are running toward a precipice." The decomposition of the word, the loss of the center: I see it expressed in this sense by this second culture.

It is important to separate the culture that subscribes to this false freedom from the culture that has called us to true liberty—or, at the very least, has pointed out the lack of true liberty, that reveals to us the void we face, that reveals our nostalgia. I believe that it is this culture of yesterday and today that interests us. It may interest us only as the witness to a cry, to a desperation, as a witness to attempting to live an impossibility.

I would like to add one last observation: what we have called the original "clump of cells" is always something physical. As I have always had a physical perception of having been a clump of cells, so I have always had a physical perception of the interiority to which this refers, of the divine interiority of this clump.

At a certain point I had that perception and it was painful and even—why shouldn't I say it?—bleeding. That perception coincided with a sign, a true and proper bruise, as if I had a fingerprint here on my forehead, in my brain, a stain. In some moments I have also cursed that stain, a stain I was not able to remove. I ended up thinking that it corresponded to the baptismal anointing. Instead, now, I know that it was and is something that came before.

LG: Before what?

GT: Before my baptism. The first baptism is the interiority of that clump of cells: this stain that is not really a stain but a *sign*—a sign (today I am able to say it) of love and of infinite freedom, a caress.

LG: It is the relationship with God that is constitutive of being.

GT: Yes, for me this perception is truly physical. I repeat that I felt it here, when I made the life I made—I felt it on my forehead, under the skin, on the bone. What is this thing? I asked myself. And then, to put it badly, I added to it the anointing of baptism, of confirmation—I added to it the sacraments that had been, so to speak, revealed to me. But in truth, since then, I believe I felt it more than understood it—that it had to do with a preceding event, that it had to do with a seal I couldn't escape, because it was itself the way out, the escape.

LG: Only that before it was all chained and confused within you. Chained and confused from a condition of the will—that is, of the energy of relationship with our being and with others—that was falsified. In short, it was what Christianity calls original sin. You were like a child locked in the basement. But in those conditions the whole house cannot and could never be calm.

LOSING OUR MEMORY

GT: And is this house the Church? Is it the world? Is it creation?

LG: How so?

GT: I mean the house that can no longer be calm. The parable of the lost sheep comes to mind. Maybe it is the Church in the world, that house. Excuse me. I must have jumped too far ahead. Starting over to connect things: is not original sin the failure to recognize oneself as being wanted?

LG: Yes, it is loving oneself by oneself—it is forgetfulness. I feel the need to insist on another Christian word: memory. What you were saying is like the total loss of memory, therefore the forgetfulness of being loved, for which one substitutes the presumption of loving ourselves by ourselves. I may think it is enough to love myself by myself—at first this might not seem to be an explicit negation of the Father, of God. But in reality it is the negation of the Father, not the negation of God as an abstract entity. Except that the negation of the Father—practically, immediately, and theoretically—becomes the negation of God. It is a negation of one's proper consistency in being a child—that is, in being loved and wanted. It is the weapon of Satan's lie.

The correct description of original sin is forgetfulness—the weapon of Satan is forgetfulness. The smoke screen in which he unleashes the lie is forgetfulness, the loss of memory. And thus the loss of memory is more and more the essence of this culture, this culture that wants to be atheist. Solzhenitsyn insists on this. In short, that substitute for the Father which is the state—in today's situation—does everything it can to cancel memory, through its slogans and through the bureaucratic nature of its thought.

GT: Returning for a moment to original sin: the fact that the first consequence of this failure to recognize ourselves as children is a sin has always given me a feeling of terrible dismay. The first consequence, the first terrible gesture committed by man after refusing to be a child of the Father, is a murder.

LG: Yes, the first meaningful gesture of that story is precisely a murder.

GT: The loss of memory, of the awareness of being wanted, immediately becomes the killing of man.

LG: To love oneself by oneself coincides with the killing of the other. But this is structural: the love of oneself by oneself always coincides with the murder of the other.

GT: Which is first (or at the same time) the forgetfulness of the other.

LG: Yes, the forgetfulness of the other. In fact, the love of a man for a woman, the love for our children, and our social life today, are all set up like this. The killing of the supreme symbol generates the forgetfulness of the other that then, practically and daily, becomes the instrumentalization of the other.

GT: And so the reduction of the other to an object. I would like to return to that first gesture, the murder: the greatest gesture of hate. In my experience, I have always seen that the direction of my hate is always toward the one whose life is more fully aware of being a child. So, in the case of the first murder, I think that the hatred was toward the one who had the sense of being a child, and the suppression happened because the presence of the one who had in himself accepted and glorified the sense of being a child could not determine the memory of the one who committed the crime.

LG: This is colossal....

GT: A circle that is broken with Cain and that then is closed and redeemed only with Christ who there, upon the Cross, says as if in witness: *Mother, behold your son.* The circle is recomposed only with the death and resurrection of Christ. Until that time, it had never been able to be remade. Anyway, it is certain that hatred is always toward the one who gives witness, toward the one who remembers, toward the one who is the memory and the living testimony of this being wanted. Man has a jealousy and envy toward the one who is richer, but hatred is reserved always and only for a man who is better than him. Hatred is always and only reserved for the helpless, toward the one who does not want to be a superman, but has accepted the state of humility and even the humiliation of being and remaining a child.

LG: And so hatred is an armed attack on memory or on the one who recalls us to memory.

GT: But don't you think that, in our time, hatred has undergone an evolution, an ultimate degradation, certainly a mechanization and abstraction without precedent? Today, true hatred is this forgetfulness.

LG: Hatred toward the one who reminds you?

GT: No. I meant to say that true hatred today is the forgetfulness of the object of hatred and of the reason for hatred. Having thus forgotten for so long, having thus sought for so long to lose the memory of his being loved, man has become capable of transforming hatred and forgetfulness into indifference, which is the most terrible form of hatred because you are not even responsible anymore for the gesture of strangling, of killing. It deceives you into calming yourself down because you avoid the gesture, because it has become mechanical.

This is the drama today: the lack of physical atrocity, of paid atrocity. Distancing ourselves from the Father, we distance ourselves also from the physical awareness of evil and substitute it with indifference. We seek, in short, to have no more contact with that clump of cells, not even in the moment when we cancel it and kill it. This is a curse on the path that a certain culture has undertaken. To kill with a sword, to kill with a knife. Then, little by little, the weapon with which you kill distances you from the man you want to strike. This is already less responsible. In this way, we fail to recognize the awfulness of killing a child of God like us. But today, from the revolver and the machine gun we have passed to the possibility of killing with gas, with atomic bombs, with poisons. It is truly a death that leaves you with clean hands. This is a terrible thing and is part of the process of this culture that has separated itself from that initial clump of cells. Do you feel like this?

LG: Yes, because it is true that indifference, neutrality, and forgetfulness are always capable of turning into hatred.

GT: For me, they are already hatred. They are the most involved form of hatred. They no longer want to assume the weight, the remorse, of hatred. They are the ultimate form and the most obscene, because they imply the loss of physical awareness of having been a clump of cells and they try to substitute that clump with a piece of plastic.

LG: They cannot cover their nature for long—sooner or later it comes out clamorously that it is hatred.

GT: But it is a hatred that tries to spare itself, to keep its hands clean—

LG: Pure Phariseeism.

GT: Something even more terrible still. Think about a man who kills a hundred, a thousand, ten thousand men with a knife, with a sword, with a blade. At a certain point he can't do it any longer; he cannot bear it. The other day, speaking of this impossibility, I read, in relation to a discussion about abortion, the report of a few doctors.

LG: Abortionists.

GT: Abortionists, yes. The report made you understand well how man cannot completely offend himself, forget himself, or make himself plastic. It said in fact that these doctors were no longer able to support the growth of the number of those killed and that they along with their assistants—

LG: Where did you read it?

GT: In *Avvenire*, the day before the article about Mother Teresa came out in the *Corriere*. These doctors said that they, along with their assistants, in order to continue the killing, would have to undergo a kind of "psychological cleansing." They would have to free themselves in the first place from the inability to continue and then to become able to bear those killings.

This triggers another difficulty: a doctor that certainly voted for abortion, who then puts that vote into practice, after a certain number of these "terminations" can no longer bear to participate directly, physically, and therefore concretely in the crime. While the person who does not participate directly in performing abortions, but only makes ideological statements about it, can continue to pride himself on having proposed, pushed, and made this law win.

THE RETREAT INTO ABSTRACTION

GT: At this point we come to a topic that is linked to all the others and that forms a characteristic of modern culture and seems to have even touched the life of Christians: that is, abstraction. We cannot calculate how much destruction, how much death, how many crimes, how many killings, happen through abstraction. But what is abstraction? It is the attempt to reduce the initial clump of cells, that is, the clump that is totally sacred and divine, the clump that proceeds, develops, grows, becomes a child, a young person, an adult, a worker, a student, a professional, a father, a mother, who has children or not—anyway it is *he* and *she*, that *he* and *she* that God willed to be a precise, unique, unrepeatable clump of soul, of flesh, and of grace. That clump of cells that is reduced by thinking of it only as a clump of material—an attempt that is still not able to take from him the presence of God, of the Eternal, of the Total, because that presence cannot be eliminated.

This is a process that is moving more and more quickly, where the clump is no longer recognized even in an exclusively materialist sense. But for this culture, as for all similar cultures, the clump of cells without God is a non-clump, a non-life, a non-human. So we have arrived by necessity to an abstract culture, a culture that says it cares about man, because it is the only alibi that it has. In reality, it proceeds against man and against itself.

Today this is where we are. The process of progress, of science, and of all the disciplines—which also could be and could still return to being for the glory of God and of man and thus develop toward the eternal history that God has given us—that process, deprived of its center, of its totality, that is to say, depleted, split, reduced to four cells, of which we do not recognize even the logic, the love, the desolation, the intelligence—this process of progress came quickly to the point of destroying the clump itself.

Yes, we have truly arrived at the crucial point in the life of man, which affects the very possibility of man's resistance and existence. Together with this, the discourse reconnects to the position of young people—young people who say no to this culture; who say no, even by killing themselves; or who say no by praying, by accepting, by rediscovering the fact that they are loved.

The point remains: the culture has escaped from the hand of the culture: the cells that we wanted to consider as a clump without God, in which there was no Father— therefore no longer as an act of love and creation—have created their own curse. They have repeated in themselves the gesture of Cain. The cells have escaped from the cells. They have created cancerous cells that man, alone, if he continues in this supposed independence—in this presumed independence from the Father—is no longer able to dominate. I don't know if you see that even in the world, the powers are losing their face. The faces of those in power no longer exist.

Look at the power of industry. Before there was a world of industry that had its face: the workers saw it with that face—it was always a real human relationship. Now, in industry, there is no longer the face of the boss, of the industrial businessman. There are these enigmatic, abstract, and terrible acronyms—ENEL, UNIDAL. Who are they? There is no longer Mr. Motta, Mr. Alemagna. There is this power without a physiognomy that has fled from every place, from concreteness, whether individual or collective.

The curse is truly this: that the cells of man, trying to take themselves away from the One from whom it is impossible to take oneself away, have become an abstraction—therefore, they generate a continual abstraction. Even in the great powers, power always coincides less with the face of the one who nominally holds it: the face of Carter, the face of Brezhnev. It is no longer like it was some ten years ago. You could still see Kennedy; you could still see Stalin. They were what they were, but they still had their faces.

Today we proceed to powers that no longer have physical faces, faces in which the memory of man can recognize itself, however distorted or disfigured. Having wanted to take away the reality of being children— and therefore the presence, the seal, the imprint of the Father—the political powers have also become machines—monstrosities, abstractions.

So, yes, it is right to recall ourselves continually to the risks of armaments, but the true risk is something other, something that lies behind the armaments. We are responsible for having lost the relationship of filiation and the awareness of the soul. So a culture that claims to be born from man as a historic event, as a historic act, has transformed itself into a culture outside of history. This culture will try to produce history and men from the abstraction of history and man. What could be more abstract than this? Then we are indignant if the majority of practical and economic resources that rationally should be used so that everyone can live, be nourished, be clothed, have a family, love, know, cultivate, are wasted on arms!

As Léo Ferré said in one of his songs, at a certain point the bombs, if they are made, must also fall. This moment—the moment of their falling and of their conflagration—is understood, whether we want to recognize it or not, on the level of mechanism, of the abstract power that constructs them. All this does not have a destiny, not even a blindly historical one, not even a blindly materialistic one. It is a frightening mechanism that operates outside of man, against man, for the destruction of man.

LG: There could even be a universal cataclysm without being able to place the blame or the responsibility on anyone.

GT: In the abstract and in the concrete, we no longer have someone to whom we can say: "It was you, it was you." Even some of our companions in the faith want to tell us that to think and to write like this is to be outside of history. I ask myself—with all respect and love for these Christians—if they know what history is. History is the slow and painful building up of man for his return to the Father. What is being done today is not construction; it is a preparation for destruction, and the destruction is not prepared without preparing also the terms in which this destruction will come.

The terrible thing is that all this happens in the abstract. People will die, but no one will have their hands dirty with blood and no one will say: "It was me; it was us." No, it will have been a mechanism. Then it is useless for them to tell us that we risk sounding apocalyptic. We, if anything, are warning about a risk—rather of *the* risk. But the one who has prepared the way for this apocalypse, the one who continues to prepare the way for it, is this abstract culture, to whom it no longer matters if power has its own face, in whom professed ideologies no longer exist, because neither Russia, nor China, nor America have real ideologies. There is now only a machine disguised as ideology. To hold on to their power (a materialist power that has become an anti-material power), they are constrained to take revenge on the One who by nature does not take revenge but embraces everything—that is to say, the Father, the Spirit, and the Son.

These powers prepare death without giving it the name of death. We are truly at a point of anti-love, anti-charity, anti-hope, anti-matter—because it is the destruction of love, charity, hope, and matter and without the desire to hear the cry of matter any longer. But the destruction of everything that comes from the Father is the destruction of everything that is a child, of everything that is living.

This is the true curse of estrangement from the Father. The curse is not the young people who die from drugs. These are a testimony to the curse—maybe they are already its fruit. In them there is a pain, and therefore, there is also an awareness and a nostalgia for that initial, bloody clump of cells—a nostalgia for the soul. The curse is in this mechanism, in this terrible network against which the battle can only be, totally and exclusively, that of love—of love for man, therefore, for the Father, for the Son, and for the Holy Spirit. There is nothing but this, this love. There is nothing but the recognition of this original filiation. In order to go forward again, we need to turn back and touch this origin.

Here is the enormous difficulty. When Pope John Paul says, "Open wide the doors to Christ. Do not be afraid," he says that we need to open wide the doors to the breaking-in of this moment in which God works in us. Because matter cannot be anything but sacred. It is, by nature, sacred. If we will rise again, this means that matter is also already able to be consecrated here, in history, even if it will have to pass through shattered bones and through ashes. If the Pope cries out like this, it is because in the cry "open wide the doors" there is the reconstitution of the meaning of *door*—the doors that existed one time in the city, the doors of a house, and above all the first door, that of the maternal womb.

This is the invitation to become aware again of matter as a divine reality. We have arrived at this: that Christians must take matter in their hands again, because matter, which for the Christian is exalted, has instead been humiliated, manipulated, annulled. The humiliated bones are those of all human beings, and we must never tire of perceiving ourselves as children.

FREEDOM & THE RECOVERY
OF RESPONSIBILITY

LG: In short, the concreteness of one's own person is freedom. The supreme urgency of this moment is precisely the recovery of responsibility—that is, the response to the Father that is called freedom, that is the life of the person. If this, beyond being unpopular, seems like it does not matter at all to this great mechanism we spoke about earlier—that mechanism that cancels all faces and that can even lead us to the total destruction of the world without anyone finding their hands dirty—even if, therefore, we are talking about something unpopular, something without recompense, and therefore an attitude that is absolutely gratuitous—well, it is this that is necessary.

Paradoxically, the little David of a liberated person stands up against the Goliath of the state, which is the powerful instrument of this mechanism that destroys man. For me, this is the sign of the times for Christians. The recovery of the memory that reconstitutes the person and thus gives space to freedom: this is necessary even if from the point of view of human expectation it is on the one hand absolutely unpopular and on the other hand without any possibility of victory. It is on this fragility—this ultimate weakness of the truth—that the power of God inserts itself with its promise. After all, the whole world has a marvelous example in the Russian dissidents, the religious Russian dissidents. Not for nothing are they totally censured by the Western culture, even from the political point of view.

GT: Referring to what you said before…at a certain point, you said: this mechanism is the instrument of the state.

LG: I said: it is the state.

GT: Now I ask you: has the situation not gone further? Let's say a word that must no longer be said, even according to certain Christians: the Antichrist, the demon, Satan. Has he been allowed to take another step? In short, does the state exist still or has the wheel turned further? From what I understand, and I say it with fear, it has already gone further.

LG: The state as a power abstracted from life is the instrument of this process.

GT: I think the state has already been consumed by the instrument.

LG: It is a type of state which no longer has a personality.

GT: It is the instrument of the one who has taken hold of it. It is a process that continually kills, descended from that first killer.

LG: It remains, anyway, the mechanism where the Antichrist acts.

GT: I have the perception that the mechanism has already escaped from the hands of the state as well—that it has already created a super-state. And the state is no longer able to control the super-state. It is no longer the true puppeteer—the true puppeteer is that mechanism that I called "total abstraction." Which is a lack of soul, which is a lack of birth, which is a lack of matter, which is a lack of love, intelligence, wisdom, judgment, equality—and, in the end, of feeling and of beauty.

In terms of non-compliance, you gave the example of the religious non-compliance in Russia and in the countries of the East. I have felt this non-compliance, I must tell you, from the time when my life brought me into a more direct, more complete, and more responsible relationship with young people—I feel it in our relationship, too. That is, the non-compliance to this mechanism.

LG: A redemption against this mechanism.

GT: Yes, I feel it strongly. Even if it is not able to assert itself. And yet we can already give it names—these names that scare those who are within the mechanism and are swallowed up in it. I am not speaking just about the case of some party. There are so many within it, too many, and they are confused. They play this terrible game together, or maybe, they begin to suffer it too. But the "no"—and I go back again to the beginning—the no of young people seems to me, even in its brutal iterations, a decided and decisive no.

LG: Theirs is a no against the absence, without ever having tasted the presence. Whereas in Russia, because in Russia it was born from young people too, the religious dissent has been the no to an absence that had already rediscovered the presence.

GT: I think because in Russia the no has been felt as more real, more physical than here with us.

LG: And in fact, they went to prison camps. The birthplace was there—in the gulag.

GT: While here the no can get tripped up by the glitter of consumption.

LG: The no here *uses*. The no lives from the same instruments that give man the absence.

GT: So here it is more difficult. There it is more painful, here it is more difficult—above all it is more difficult to have an active conscience. To say no here is more difficult because the mechanism that overwhelms you furnishes you continually with myths, with momentary illuminations—therefore, to give flesh and body to the no is harder here. But it seems very important to me that there be this will of opposition.

LG: Yes, as a general inclination. But there is also this terrible limit, this *etouffement* [suffocation]—how to say it?

GT: This continual fall. With the risk then that, because of the mechanism, the opposition will become more muted, more deadened.

LG: That's why I said *etouffé*, suffocated....

GT: At this point, the only path of liberation is to give the "no" the face of a "yes," to give the "no" the face of consent to being wanted.

LG: To give the no a memory. This is the rediscovery.

GT: And it is here, I think, that the Cross stands. I don't think any other solution is possible. The Cross that, for example, in Russia has been and is the gulag, and here, in one way or another, would have to be taken up.

LG: This is the fear that comes, because it is a real possibility. It is like in the Bible—when they were complacent, God sent the flood. Something has to happen. This is so true that the call to memory is not always received, not even by those who should be the army of this memory. This is so true that the call to memory comes off like a nuisance or is accused of naïveté, of "integralism." The abstract dominates even over the will to remember, over the recovery of memory. So much theology nowadays, so much Catholic education—

GT: —is done *a latere*, is done above and outside.

LG: It is done outside of life. The word of the Pope strikes but does not shake.

THE REAWAKENING OF THE PERSON

GT: Maybe even the one who feels shaken is pretending, because here there can also be a process of simulation. But this pretending is becoming the instrument of cancellation and of suppression. Except that no one can avoid the fact that man is made of soul and of flesh.

LG: Therefore, we need to give back to these things the name of murder. Because the word "murder" is stronger than words like "indifference" or "suppression" or "marginalization." We need to maintain that the impulses of this culture are often impulses to murder. The word murder is that which by antithesis can reawaken the awareness of the person. Because this is the time of the rebirth of personal awareness. It is as if we can no longer make organized crusades or movements.

A movement is born with the reawakening of the person. It is something striking. I was making the comparison before to David and Goliath. It is precisely the person who, in front of a mechanism like you described, is the most ridiculous thing—the most laughable thing that can be, with no possibility of success—precisely this person is the point of redemption. And this is how the concept of a movement is born. The most valuable social reality now for a counterattack is the ideal of a movement, which exists as if it did not have head or tail, we don't know how it happens. In fact, its point of birth is in the most inexperienced and unarmed particle that exists: that is, the person.

GT: But it is at this point that the re-flowering of the person, in an irresistible way, intervenes, which is then the re-flowering of memory: that is to say, the re-flowering of being loved. Defenseless, maybe already beaten at the start—excuse me if I say "maybe," but I am certain that the love of God is greater than all the mechanisms and all the abstractions.

LG: No, "maybe." It is exactly the way God wins. Only that for God *a thousand years are as a single day.* God wins according to his time. And this is for us the Cross. Because even for Christ the Cross, according to the measure of that society, was the non-victory.

GT: It is the Cross, as you say, but it is also hope.

LG: The main problem is to reignite the mastery that the person has over himself, to revive the person, to recover the meaning of birth. It cannot be a discourse, a debate. The true problem is the resurgence of the person. And this is a Sisyphean task because, even if everyone waits for this, still, at one time—before being at the mercy of the mechanism that crushes everything and dissolves everything because it desacralizes everything, before being free from this mechanism—the person has to be found again. In this sense it is a word that must run, that must communicate itself, that must not let us sleep, that must catalyze hope. And it is a task whose original point seems so small, minute, capillary—and capillary in the ultimate sense of the word, because it is in the singular.

People who are abandoned, people who have been stripped of the sacredness of their origin, of their constitution, are scattered because they are easily manipulated. How do we pull them from this terrible gravitational force, from the power of the terrible catalyzing force that the instruments of this mechanism have?

GT: By starting with man in his pain, in the extreme point where today he has been left to fall—the point of death. A suicidal person, who no longer wants to live, who desires death, comes to you. You find him there; he announces himself to you; you come across him in the street. It doesn't matter how—you encounter him, and even if he doesn't say it to you, he wants to end his life. What do you do?

He knocks on your door. He comes to you because he has to tell you certain things before ending his life, before completing that gesture against his life, that life from which memory and meaning have been taken. And I imagine that if one arrives there, he is cut down, overcome by nostalgia. You open the door. He is there. What do you do?

LG: I don't know how to respond to you, because in that moment I say what I can and in the way I can.

GT: If he, or she, enters, looks at you—which means that she still, as I believe, desires to see you—

LG: If they come, they have a need to see....

GT: This look of theirs means something, which is the last foothold that remains. Maybe you have experienced this.

LG: Yes, it is a small minority that expresses itself like this. But the words of this minority can touch the masses.

GT: They are like the darkest point but also the most acute—the point that expresses all the others. The first thing that happens is that they need to cry. Who today would refuse a person the right to cry, the right to cry as liberation? They cry in order to re-acquire their memory, the possibility of a memory. The abstraction in which we live is at fault for this as well: for not letting people cry anymore, for making man unlearn how to cry while causing him to cry. But that which is allowed today is no longer a cry for liberation. Is it not rather another terrible effect of this abstraction that has taken from man even the liberation that comes from crying and left him only the humiliation of tears, tears that no longer restore the confidence of life and even of death?

LG: This is tragic because it is only a different presence that can interrupt this logic, this mechanism. Those people there—

GT: Those people, many people, all people. Those people there are the extreme cases, the signs of an unease that has come to the edge of a cliff.

LG: If the fault lies with the abstraction, then it is only the concrete that can undermine this dominion of abstraction. And the concrete is a different presence. But a different presence is expressed in words, in words that allow a glimpse of continuity—not words that define, in the sense that this world defines everything, which means that they make everything a corpse. Therefore these words must express a living content—in other words, a presence.

I am unable to find a sign of hope other than the multiplying of people who are presences—the multiplying of these people and an inevitable sympathy or (to put it somewhat awkwardly) a new kind of "union" among them. We use the term "recognition" to express this. Outside of this, the path is so poor, the human is so confined, it is as if the homeless in a city should do combat with the power that rules the city.

We need to have the courage of the truth of ourselves—the small courage of the truth of ourselves. This means the awareness that desperation is a lie, a lie that can be conquered in ourselves, but that cannot be conquered by society, by an army, even an army of conscientious objectors. Desperation must first be conquered in ourselves. This comes only from the rebirth of the self. And so I say: "Understand that killing yourself will not resolve anything, because your soul remains. Do not avoid tomorrow; you cannot avoid destiny—destiny is greater than you, and, in fact, you did not exist and then you were born. Therefore you are within something greater than what is hurting you, than what is persecuting you, than what is withering you. And what constitutes you, your destiny, has the ability to raise you up if you only desire it, if you only accept it."

In this sense, I say to all these people that the first thing to do is something that may seem strange: to pray. I always use the example of the character known as "The Unnamed" from Alessandro Manzoni's novel, *The Betrothed*: "God, if you exist, reveal yourself to me."

Because this is the point. And this does not only hold for the desperate person, but for anyone; this is the thing that I say to all the kids.

GT: It is possible also to suggest that one way of saying, "If you exist, reveal yourself to me" is to hate yourself a little less—I mean, as creatures of God, to want a little bit more good for yourself. That man might love himself a little more, not as something unconnected but as a creature of God, that is, as a man who is connected, loved, wanted, and therefore, eternal.

LG: Certainly.

GT: "Love yourself more, because loving yourself more you will recognize that you have been wanted by love." Maybe it is the love that has loved us that pushes us to love ourselves right there on the edge of the volcano, on the edge of the cliff.

LG: The problem is right here. And also the problem is how to get there. Because once we arrive at this fruit, we begin to eat.

GT: "Esteemed more than the nothing to which you have been reduced, you are greater, you are more important, you are more ineradicable."

LG: Or like a manifesto of some university students who proclaimed: "Life is greater." There it is.

GT: Every man and woman participates in this greatness. Therefore, the greater life is, the greater humanity is. These two greatnesses are indivisible, one makes the other greater.

LG: Yes, but life does not exist if you are the source of that life. For me, the point is to go back to the evidence that our life is not born from ourselves, but belongs to something greater, and it is this something greater that constitutes us.

GT: Which is not separable from your life—which is the determining depth of your life.

I CANNOT SAY "I"
IF I DO NOT SAY "YOU"

LG: Something greater constitutes us. This means the discovery of the paradox that I am an Other. I cannot say "I" if I do not say "you," if I do not say "you who make me." This is what I affirm when I try to explain what prayer is. What I wanted to say at the beginning of this part of our dialogue is that the lie dominates—as Jesus said: *the whole world is subjected to the lie*. Now the lie has reached its complete paradox because life's concreteness is cancelled. But the lie plays itself out in the person. In fact, one kills himself or lives as a dead person, giving himself up for dead—this, then, is the true suicide. So it is still in the person that the retrieval, the resurgence, the revolution plays out. And yet, how does this recovery happen now? This is the point to look at. The only response is that you encounter a different presence. This presence can then act as a reactant, as the catalyst of man's dispersed energies.

GT: It must reawaken the sense of birth.

LG: Exactly. And the reawakening of memory happens in the company of one who already lives this memory. There is no other solution. It is the multiplication of these presences. The Bible says: *to every man God has given the responsibility of his brother*: one who has faith even in a simple, implicit way cannot help but preserve his faith in what is human. He must therefore care about the people who surround him and become a presence for those who are close by—first of all, for a husband, a wife, for children, for friends at school, university classmates, coworkers. But if this reawakening proves itself true, it is impossible for these people not to recognize each other, not to establish a solidarity, not to feel a need arising among them, as I said before, a "union."

It is from the multiplication of these atoms that a movement arises, a movement that offers an answer to the mechanism of power. But the type of drying up in which people grow up today, the type of nihilism that society generates, stunts the retrieval of responsibility that is had by those who preserve the faith, even in those who preserve a natural faith in the value of life. Therefore this nihilism makes it almost impossible for a movement to be born today. Anyway, this is the fundamental aspect of a counterattack in today's society—that the truth, which lives in my person, in my very "I," becomes reanimated, that it have the courage of its being, of its life, that it realize itself.

GT: And that it understands the necessity to communicate—

LG: —to understand the human strength that it has, the responsibility to spread this awareness throughout creation in its relationship with others. So it is important that those who have experienced this recovery of awareness of the person not refuse solidarity with others who have had the same fortune, the same grace. Which, in turn, means that they do not refuse to feel themselves a part of the divine movement in the world.

GT: If they refuse, would it mean that they no longer have it? In short, that they are already losing the sense of memory? In effect, memory must not refuse to recognize others that live within the same memory of the origin, of birth.

LG: I agree, and this is the true tragedy of Christians. Today they are a bit like flickering wicks of that memory. It is a shame that they are incapable of recognizing the unity that exists among them—that is, the communion that is immanent in their life.

GT: And they are incapable of recognizing also the signs that grace sends with extraordinary abundance. And so I believe that, returning to what you said earlier, to the man who encounters one who already recognizes this memory in himself and who creates a bond with him: I think that man can recover the possibility of this memory also in an encounter with nature. In short, the sign of creation is powerful and illuminating there, too.

LG: A few weeks ago, I met a young man who wrote me and said that he truly felt himself a man only when he was walking in nature, among the fields.

GT: The encounter with nature, then. Nature is also a place of memory: the encounter can also happen there. A memory that grows and that maybe cannot perceive the intensity with which it exists, a memory in which man can see himself and recognize himself. I don't know if you have ever thought about why, when we live or when we pass through certain moments of the day, why we feel with the most acute subtlety this memory of being created, this presence of being created, to the point of almost noticing a kind of laceration, a wound. In fact, memory, as we have said, can also be painful.

Have you ever asked yourself why, when you find yourself within a moment in nature that is so miraculous and you tremble at it, you feel this reawaking as an expansion of the sign of God, the sign of creation—and you feel yourself growing as if an organ were accompanying a single voice? Why does this happen? Is it not in those moments that the memory of a total unity is experienced in which nature also participates?

I believe equally that this encounter with memory can happen even through the signs of culture, through works that man has left within history—books, music, the forms of art. Even from there a restoration of the sign of being children, of being loved, can come.

The field of possibility is therefore infinite. The problem is that we Christians are used to limiting it, we are almost unable to read the signs that grace sends us—signs that can be happy or painful; that can be, for example, the light that is showing now in the air, there, outside the window—or it can be, instead, a sickness. We are not more open, more on the lookout. What are we defending ourselves from, then? Our aridity, I think.

Instead, the Christian must offer himself entirely, abandon himself to God. I believe that the abundance of grace is infinite, above all today. But we don't know how to read this grace for ourselves and thus we don't know how to open it for others. When we think we have read it and we help others read it, it is often with meanings that are partial, incomplete. We can and should use the terms of science, of literature, of philosophy, and rise up through them to the origin of those signs, to the origin of memory—in short, to birth—and thus grasp their meaning, and together, let ourselves be grasped by it.

LG: What you say is very good, but I insist that the catalytic encounter with a human presence is almost inevitable—otherwise a sense of dependence can emerge that does not lead to the discovery of our own person. Without the catalytic encounter with a human presence, everything gets out of focus, as happens to one who is undone by a sense of panic in reality. Instead, contact with the documents of human history—art, music, literature—certainly point to a presence. But the moment always comes when there has to be another person present.

I simply wanted to say that the hope that I live and that so many others live with me is not a gullibility, nor an undervaluing of the cynicism in which everything is immersed. But it is the example of a life that begins to move the ice, that begins to warm the body, the body that has been frozen. And this must be multiplied, becoming a socially relevant phenomenon, a mutual recognition, a mutual companionship—this is the process instituted by Christ. There have been people that have rediscovered their origin, their destiny, by contact with his person—they have felt themselves brothers and sisters, a companionship and a rule for each other.

The concept of a rule in the history of the Church finds meaning—before it is a codification of its articles—in a companionship toward destiny. This is the phenomenon that should happen, without demanding labels, membership cards, and it should happen everywhere that a person moves. From this point of view, the Church is a marvel, because despite the betrayal of clerics and the great forgetfulness of her children, she remains the true presence of people in friendly connection as a companionship toward destiny, where the richness of the companionship is memory, where the companionship becomes a school of memory. And the place of memory is when one says "I."

GT: I in You.

LG: The place of memory is when one says "I," discovering that this I is an Other, that this I is constituted by the presence of something other. Saint Augustine says that prayer is *elevatio mentis in Deum* [raising the mind to God], the awareness of oneself all the way to its original point. I in You, because in history it is said that you became one of us, to make yourself felt, to make yourself seen....

GT: To make a way for me to say "I." And I could pronounce that word only when You became man.

LG: *Come to me all you who labor and are burdened and I will give you rest.* Christians must become again this place of memory.

GT: Why have you said that the kind of participation in the cosmos in which we become children from time to time is a kind of pantheism? Is it possible—not speaking only in a literary way—that there is a resurrection for nature? The blood of Christ that is the blood of the incarnate Son, who was oppressed, whipped, wounded, murdered—is it possible that this does not become more precise, more illuminated, and possibly more glorious if you see its sign also in a plant that rises up in the sun or in a sunset that spreads over the houses of a city?

LG: I did not mean to say this: come on! The cosmos is the first sign of God. Nor on the other hand did I mean to diminish the tragic testimony of suffering, death, persecution, injustice: they are evocative moments.

But you first asked me the question: "If someone came to you that wanted to call it quits, if he knocked on your door...." I cannot speak to this person about the cosmos—I cannot say, multiplying indefinitely his problem, that "there are millions of people who are torn, crushed, and you are an emblem of this." I was speaking from a pedagogical point of view. In order to make the aversion of our humanity in front of injustice something stable and clear, we need a man who catalyzes all this— we need a person. And thus, the good of this world comes from multiplying these people in a companionship that they recognize among themselves.

If the companionship is refused it means that also the initial emotion will languish. I don't remember the novel well, but in *Doktor Faustus* by Thomas Mann there is a composer, Leverkühn, who walks away from home to affirm his autonomy and then goes crazy. The only thing that he decides, in the last glimmer of intelligence and clarity that remains to him, is to return to his mother.

GT: There is a phrase in Novalis: "Philosophy is nostalgia: the desire to return home." This is the concept of memory that you are speaking of and that I would call the sense of birth. It is something that concentrates all that we have been saying.

LG: I was only outlining a method for this nostalgia to spread out again. But the protagonist is the individual, the person: and the fabric is woven by the person multiplying himself in a companionship.

GT: Woven in love, by necessity.

THE SIGN OF A COMPANIONSHIP

LG: There is a fundamental factor that we have not highlighted, and it is grace.

GT: Maybe there is a hint of this grace in the signs that cannot be calculated, that we can never predict—how they arrive, from whence they arrive, nor when they arrive. Here the conversation that we have already had comes back in. The mechanism that overwhelms us and that crushes us builds huge walls between man and grace. It puts terrible obstacles between man and the infinite descending of grace. We do not love each other enough, do not dedicate ourselves enough so that first of all those who have grasped the meaning of birth recognize each other, so that loving each other they might multiply. So this not dedicating ourselves to each other is already like helping to build those walls, that "no."

LG: Especially since we cannot censure with impunity the fact that the origin—that of which we are made—has become a companionship: the first presence that moved in the world, the first push toward this saving companionship of the person, is a permanent presence in life.

GT: I think the Incarnation happened to make us recognize everyone as family.

LG: As a companionship.

GT: *I will be with you until the end of days.*

LG: And this is revealed as a presence within the companionship of those who recognize him, who accept him.

GT: What you call companionship exists, but in order for it to be such it has to be continually recognized, accepted, welcomed, and woven. And then it is a companionship or, as I say, a painful family.

LG: Yes, because the sign of this companionship, which is glorious and vast because He is risen, is a presence. This presence reaches man through a physical sign, which is the companionship of his followers. And it is, like you say, a painful companionship because this sign is made up of all these poor pieces, these poor faltering people. Here there is a judgment that comes from the heart of man: because the heart that desires truth recognizes the accent of the presence of truth, even through the lameness, the incoherence, the misery of the human sign. While whoever does not seek the truth in a real way, but seeks his own satisfaction, is then scandalized by the lameness, by the misery, and remains with his ears closed and does not hear the accent of truth.

GT: He no longer reads creation, no longer hears, and, as a result, he no longer speaks—he becomes blind and mute.

LG: Instead, Christ's presence strikes us as an unmistakable accent, infinitely discreet but unmistakable, that cannot be put aside without sinning. The slavery of evil is such that we run in search of a pretext to say that it is not true. It is as if we said: this is not enough for me—I want to see, I want to put my finger in the wound. The way that God reaches man is through an accent that resonates even within the forms of human misery—but often man does not welcome this accent. To justify this rejection, they take as a pretext the petty and faltering aspects of that companionship.

GT: Which is a lack of charity.

LG: It is a lack of the desire to be saved, and so also a lack of charity toward ourselves.

GT: Whereas in this recognition—in this sense of birth that is participated in and multiplied—there is nothing that is not for the good of human history.

LG: Memory is a good for history, because the recognition of our original dependence—that is, of our poverty of spirit—enables us in the end to possess the world, to perceive ourselves as part of a story full of meaning and goodness.

GT: All the infinite possibilities that exist in each person—and that exist in the grace of this specific individual—become active even as history. Thus, the memory that by the will of God becomes history is the only path by which history can become for man a passage that is painful but also constructive. The alternative, as we can see in our time, is a non-passage that is painful and destructive. Contrary to what is frequently affirmed today, history has been redeemed—it is built up and glorified by faith.

LG: From the restoration of memory in man.

GT: Reason, intelligence, science, poetry, and art are founded on the meaning of birth. The polemic that is continually made that faith is a denial of reason is not true. It is a false, abusive polemic. It is a partial reading. Because, in effect, there is nothing that is more reasonable than relying on the absolute reason of our birth.

LG: In everything that reason does, there is nothing more reasonable than this sense of belonging to a design.

GT: Not only that, but there is nothing that makes reason more reasonable than recognizing the reason within this immense and infinite design. I would say that this design is an illumination of reason—it is the height of reason as it is the height of imagination, of sensibility, and of love. All of this is stretched toward its true potential— it is the contrary of where the world is today, which is an immobility determined by its submission to the power-mechanism.

LG: Yes, it is contrary to where the world is today— precisely because he knows that everything belongs to something greater than himself, in which everything is redeemed—even the petty, even that which is by itself small and poor. So also the miserable and the painful participate in a meaning—that is, they acquire value and greatness.

The supreme concept—which is anthropologically bigger than Christianity—is the concept of *offering*. Offering is when the individual expresses himself in a gesture, however small, that represents a total participation in being. If man recognizes that he belongs to a design of God and to his will, recognizes that he belongs to Christ—even if he is stuck in bed—he becomes an indispensable part of that design. In fact, the design would be lacking something if that instant was lacking. And that design, prescinding from all its conditions, gives to that instant all the charge of its total significance—that is, of Christ himself. There is no longer anything useless, nothing unfortunate, nothing unlucky, nothing thrown out. But in all this, the value of man, whatever he does, small or great, plays out in the awareness of its relationship with everything, with God, with the Father—in the awareness of *belonging*.

GT: This awareness—this will to belong—generates pain and happiness at the same time: the happiness is given by the awareness of belonging, and the pain is the physical living-out of this belonging. It does not seem possible to take away this pain.

LG: Because this is the condition of existence and history. Pain arises when one lives belonging all the way to the death of the self. A real belonging should remain even in the instant when it requires a renunciation of the self: *Whoever loses his life will save it; whoever wants to save his life will lose it.*

GT: This pain is unavoidable, but it is the only choice that guarantees this belonging. It is possible even if man, given his misery, cannot bear this pain by his own power. There remain moments in which it becomes possible—then the height of pain coincides with the height of happiness. Even in our misery—or, as you say, lameness—there must be moments in the life of every man and woman when he or she says "yes," in which the maximum perception of pain and powerlessness—the maximum sensation of not being able to bear it, the maximum perception of misfortune and of death—end up coinciding with maximum happiness. And here I mean happiness as awareness of belonging.

LG: Like a powerless baby who relaxes completely when his mother takes him in her arms.

GT: When you recognize entirely and wholly your nothingness—when you feel your fall, your ashes, your bones, your very coffin—in that moment you perceive the greatest awareness that is given us, the greatest happiness, if that happiness is, as I believe, awareness.

LG: It is the possibility of joy. Saint Paul says: *I abound with joy in my tribulations*. But you are saying something else. You are saying that even the most tragic experience of my nothingness, of my evil—if I recognize it—becomes a cry of pain that coincides with the certainty of a presence. And therefore it becomes hope.

GT: It becomes happiness. Happiness in a complete, total sense. But the notion of happiness in society today does not lead to an awareness of our limits—it flees from this continually in order not to have recognize and consider our human limitations.

LG: At the price of forgetfulness. It is the propaganda of power—

GT: —maybe a seduction.

LG: In any case, it is the art of forgetfulness. Happiness is human when it does not come at the price of forgetfulness.

OFFERING & EXCHANGE

GT: To return to the instance of someone who opens your door and tells you that he wants to kill himself. If he sees in your eyes that within you there is already a part of the whole—if you make him see it—in that moment the first and painful perception can begin for him. That perception, even if it is deeply painful, is of his being a son—and, therefore, of his birth. For the person who comes to the ultimate point of desperation and pain, by the way you look at him—how you find yourself in front of and within him—you become not just some other, but the other that he was seeking. You become almost a co-suicide out of love of where he has arrived.

At this point, even he, without saying anything, recognizes the definitive and liberating meaning of the relationship that has been established. All of life is held in that exchange. At this extreme point, life must become a conscious and loving exchange of roles—and of crosses. This does not mean losing one's individuality, but on the contrary, recognizing it and entrusting it to the One who is total charity—and therefore, through him, to the other. If God became one of us out of love—if he assumed our misery not for a moment but for thirty-three years, and re-assumes it every day, every hour, every moment—then the misery of the sign, which you spoke about, goes beyond the companionship. It is through the misery that Christ offers himself to us, hands himself over to us.

The difference between "union-ism" and "communion"—between "society" and "community"—can be understood here. Unionism and society put limits on relationships, they bureaucratize them; they are established and deciphered according to rights and duties. The Christian meaning of communion and of community does not limit or require anything—it allows you to correspond with the other. This communion is brought to the limit of abandonment, the point where two beings can love each other within the design of God. In them, then, there is a point in which—by a mystery that is the mystery of creation—the Spirit, God, Christ, father and mother, become a single event, a single essence.

The fullness of love and of awareness in the self at this moment identifies oneself in the need of others, in the pain of others, in the being of others without asking anything in return. It is here where we Christians are often abstract. When they asked Mother Teresa what she thought of politics and society, she replied: "I don't have time to think about these things." In this answer it becomes clear that for the Christian there is only time to encounter the person. This identification can certainly pass through politics and through society—but only pass through, not be limited by it, not treating that passage as a total, definitive place.

In my experience I have always seen that the way you look at a person—whether he comes to seek you out or you encounter him—establishes or prohibits a relationship, a human relationship. This means that we need to be and to live a little beyond the immediate expectation that other people can have of us. So if you open the door (it could be the house, the church, the street, a bar) to one who has decided to end it all, that has decided to leave, and you have the habit of the recognition, of the memory and presence of Christ, he enters and you are already there where he no longer dared to even think. (This can be said without the sin of pride because in any case it is Christ that permits you to be there.) Then he looks at you and you see that only by your look you give him the whole meaning of a life that is loved by God, and you restore him to himself—that is, to his sonship, to God.

This is what, by extension, we Christians should be doing: to be always going beyond what is requested of us. It already seems impossible to respond to what the world desperately asks us—to what the world that has been denied, strangled, diminished, the world from which the memory of birth has been cancelled, asks of us. But we can and should be there. We don't just need to be ready to respond, we need to have already in ourselves the fulfillment of the question that will be asked of us—its pain, its reasons, its extreme wounds.

LG: We need to have already responded before we can respond.

GT: Maybe the answer is contained in our daily living.

LG: We need to be already changed, in order to express the word that is asked of us.

GT: In words and gestures, which are the forms of life. And here we turn to the form of life. If the form of life is born from the recognition of our being children, of our being redeemed by Christ, it cannot be anything but a form that contemplates, and contains all the questions, all the needs of man's desperation. Charity—here is charity.

In that case, it seems that the gravest sin would be that of omission. It is not the sin of passion that is horrendous. It is the sin of omission—the sin of abstraction. It is to omit, to fail to grow and to abandon ourselves. This is the worst thing that a Christian can do: to lag behind with respect to life's questions. Or even to be in a position of no longer feeling them, these questions of the world—the questions of those who have not had the gift of recognizing this memory yet.

Because it is not that this memory no longer exists. I refuse to think that someone is not a part of love, that someone is not a part of Christ, that Christ is not in everything. It is, rather, that we do nothing, or too little, for everyone to be given the possibility to recognize it. But Christ is there—he lives, he weeps and dies, in everyone. One can kick him out; but he does not leave. He does not leave even if someone kills himself. No, I do not believe that he leaves even in that moment. Maybe the one who kills himself will be damned because he believed that he cast Christ out, but Christ was there, with him, even in that moment. Maybe Christ bent down out of infinite love right after that desperate gesture.... I don't know. Christ on the Cross does not leave; he never leaves. So it is this way of being present that is always needed in abundance.

Here is the only way to be—if it is a way of living in memory, of being not unworthy of Christ who stays with us, who pursues us and loves us. Maybe the good will sung about by the angels on the field of Bethlehem is really this. To live without memory is anti-Christian—anti-Christian as the abstraction and the abstract power that we spoke about earlier. Just think: we have the only true power, the power to participate in Christ—we can accept this gift and think of it as a shelter, our own reserve, both the place where we go hunting for truth and itself a source of life!

LG: In this sense, sin is always an attempt to live outside our human limits—always.

GT: I always find myself coming up short, even when I think I am living in the "happy medium." I know that I always have to do more, to be more, to go further. But this is where the tension, the drive, is to be found. This tension becomes a habit, in a positive sense—a habit that always re-invents itself—therefore, a habit that can never be laziness, because it must always broaden and deepen itself—and broaden and deepen you in the process. If today you are here, tomorrow you should be there.

This habit is a tension of love, of charity, and because of this, the limits are always being stretched. I would say that this habit—which is also the habit of prayer—is something of which the world has an extreme and continuous need. This continual growth is not a lump sum—the world does not need to hear it and see it all at once. But the world should be able to see this growth because it is always there, living through our suffering and our prayer for the world. In this way, everything in the world becomes an opportunity for grace. Only if we have experienced both the need that the world has and the fulfillment of that need—only if we are disposed to welcome these needs—can we avoid error. You arrive and they arrive. They arrive and you must already be there.

LG: In this way, everything becomes encounter and no longer conflict.

GT: Encounter and also donation. I think today man has a need—a tragic but also an anxious and trembling need—for someone to understand and welcome him, even before he asks to be welcomed—not because of his own merit but because of the design of God, because God has willed that man find himself beyond his own desperation. The desperation today is enormous—a huge void; a huge pain; a huge blindness—but also enormous in its need for the fullness of a true vision and a true intelligence. So the answer to this need, the home we offer, should be large enough to welcome them.

LG: That a man may feel himself welcomed by another even in his darkest desperation.

GT: That he may feel immediately that there is a brother or sister; and that this brother or sister speaks to him even before he speaks, questions, calls him or her. I think that in this sense the figure of Mary becomes a kind of home for us. Because the *yes* she said was beyond every *yes* pronounced before and after by man. What I said before about the womb, about the embrace of a home, is found here, in her.

And today's man, who is so prideful, so apparently secure—but in truth is so uncertain, lost, disheartened, wretched—needs her. From her he receives a maternal and total welcome. It is an extraordinary sign that the last two popes have re-proposed the figure of Our Lady. It is a sign of God that John Paul II does not give a homily, does not say a prayer, in which she is not invoked, the Mother of God.

LG: *Banished children of Eve*—she is a port, a home for us.

RETURNING TO
THE HOUSE OF THE FATHER

GT: The truth is that man today does not say it—maybe he is afraid to say it—but he feels a terrible nostalgia to return home to the house of the Father. And then the Mother is there, with Christ, to form the shelter, the home, the Church. From there, as I said before, I think that man can begin a total rediscovery.

For us "children" that rediscovery can only pass through Mary, through the Mother—a fact that we Christians have forgotten or even become ashamed of. Just think: we are ashamed of her, our Mother. After all, we have forgotten and are also ashamed of Christmas. Instead, this is the moment when desperate man needs to rediscover Christmas, to rediscover his own birth. To give up or forget the liturgy is a tremendous sin.

We do not fully grasp what the liturgy means, consciously and unconsciously, as it is carried out and participated in—the liturgy in which the community lives. It is something beyond what we can see and know historically. I am referring to the diffusion of grace that is in the liturgy of the Church. It is a great fault to have forgotten it and somehow restricted these moments of grace.

To return to Christmas—which in the liturgy is the moment of grace *par excellence*—the moment of the birth of Christ—man does not desire this. He leaves his house because it is no longer a home, because it has been desecrated, reduced to nothing. He may build a more decent house, but they have taken from him the memory of that other home—I mean, the shelter, the home—the absolute home of our history: the Church.

This, instead, is the moment in which man cries in nostalgia to have his own true home again and to travel and find again in its depths the true and proper Christmas: the birth of Christ. I think that these moments— because they are more humble, more heartbroken, more threatened by rhetoric and risk—are also those that must be recovered whole and entire; they must be recovered and made present again—in front of the groan, the cry, the desperation, the madness of modern man.

And how do we risk the madness, how can we free man, if we do not help him find again the meaning of that first moment, of that first cry, and then the meaning that is within, tightly bound up, the meaning of the first cry of Christ—that is, of God who, to restore this memory, became man? Not even the Passion can be read properly if it does not participate deeply in the reality that is Christmas. From the cross Christ said: *Mother, behold your son*—that is, he rebuilt the circle of the family, of the shelter, of the home, of the Church: the circle of Christmas.

There you see the heart of everything: the desire to return to the home, which is the reconquest of memory and also of the possibility of reaching the goal. Then the whole path that we must run, all the pain that there will be along this road—because there is a hard and painful road ahead—then, if you keep present the moment in which Christ was born in history, the moment in history when God brought you to birth, the moment when you were born, if you always have it present, you have in you the total reason, therefore the affective reason, the warmth and the strength to walk this road.

I do not think it can be avoided—the road that will allow man to return to Christ will be incredibly difficult, but it seems to me that the moment of the origin will be fundamental. Because it is the moment of the origin of every day, of every hour, of every minute. It is like when we say a prayer: if when you say it you don't just repeat it, but you go back to its origin, you bring it back to his birth, everything becomes new for you, everything is reborn. Then, in this sense, Christmas is making every day, every minute, every word you say, every gesture you do, the effort you make, the work you carry out, the children you bring up, the children that aren't yours, to whom you try to give everything you would give to your children—all of this is renewed, becomes a true Christmas every time, an announcement, but an announcement incarnated in the incarnation of Christ, therefore a real, total announcement.

LG: You are right: it becomes Christmas.

GT: Always, when you live it, when you create Christmas every time, in such a way that every gesture becomes Christmas, every moment becomes his birth—your birth in Him, in the Father.

LG: That everything you do would be done for the meaning that has brought you to birth again through the memory of your birth, of your origin.

GT: It is when we lose this sense that everything becomes repetition and therefore abstraction.

LG: In this way, you are no longer part of a story....

GT: Perhaps this also raises the theme of time, of its passing. If you live every moment as a fact of birth, of growth, but which is always birth, then you feel that it will always be there—that it will pass away, but it will enter and remain within everything in your experience. If you do not live like this, you get a feeling of exhaustion—then it will mean that you have not truly lived that moment.

Let's take these hours here, which we have spent talking. They will no longer exist. But they will exist forever if we have spent them in Christmas—in the Christmas of their unfolding, minute by minute. Then you already have the perception that, modestly, with all our weakness and miseries, they have no other claim than to be a Christmas for us and for everyone. Then always from the ashes in which they are reduced, you will feel that they are fixed—that we will find them there, forever.

If instead we let them fall, they become a monotony—the usual, a habit. Then you feel that they have not had a Christmas, and that they won't rise again. They will be ashes that will not rise up again. In this sense, do you think that the end, the conclusion of history, the resurrection of the body, will carry with it and contemplate all these acts, all these "birth" moments? I think there will be the effort that it cost Michelangelo to paint the Sistine Chapel, but the Sistine Chapel will no longer be there. It will not make sense for it to be there. Do you agree with this?

LG: Certainly. The human value of the Sistine Chapel will remain forever.

GT: What it cost him and the world around him to make it, as it will be for you, for me....

LG: This is what it says in the Gospel: *Every word will be accounted for.*

GT: We do not arrive there with the works in themselves and for themselves. We arrive with the strength, with the love, with the faith, with the hope that is in these works. The works are necessary moments. But then I think eternity will be made from the drive, the feelings that have determined these works, for good and for bad. I think that damnation is the awareness of the negativity of those drives and those feelings; the remorse, therefore, of those drives, those feelings, and those moments that did not participate in the total design. Therefore there will be an eternal and definitive nostalgia, of not participating in the total design, of being outside ourselves with all our moments, our hours, our years—outside the meaning of birth. Maybe we have gone too far beyond the subject of our discussion....

LG: By its nature, this type of conversation is free to go wherever.

GT: But, returning now, let me ask: what is the degree— be extremely free—of your hope in young people?

LG: It is great, because the moment seems to have come when the Lord, if he wants to save his work, must renew persons—he must bring into existence those persons, those companionships, he must create these movements of which we have spoken. The moment has come. It is like a sign of the times. Therefore, paradoxically, the moment when the crisis reaches its depth is the greatest moment of hope.

GT: Do you think that today's youth justify this hope at least as much as the young people of twenty years ago?

LG: They justify it more.

GT: But not only because they are deeper, not only because they have been allowed to go deeper....

LG: They justify it more because they are more true.

GT: Because they suffer more, because they can no longer cheat, because they are in front of an either/or. Now it is truly a question of life or death. And then because there are signs. One part of the youth, that is becoming ever greater, is already on the counterattack. It is a counterattack that is unarmed when it comes to political tactics and practical, dirty techniques, but armed in terms of—

LG: —the force of truth.

GT: The force of truth, of memory, and of charity— armed also by abandonment to Christ. I think this is a reality that already has a shape, that is already taking on a form. Because if we are here and this book begins a series of books and does not remain the only one, it is because someone, who is no longer that young, has seen, recognized, felt, been struck, shaken—someone has been moved, discovering these young people, in the hope, in the movement, in the passion, in the love of the Father and therefore of man. An integral love, decisive even in weakness: continually on the way because it is firm in this anchor that never makes you stop, but makes you go forward, always beyond. This anchor is the Cross, it is Christ. This collection of books, what we are trying to do, is thanks also to them. And the credit—which is a responsibility, I think—should be given and communicated to them, because it is right, because it belongs to them.

LG: Because of the hope that it raises up in us and in them.

GT: In us, in them, and also outside, in the desperation of the world. Then, you already know it, but maybe when we are within this hope we may not realize how profound it is, because you have been there with many of these young people, as I said at the beginning, as a brother, a father.

LG: I am a presence....

GT: If I say it to you, I might be adding to the weight you carry. You have been there and you can always be there more. See, Giussani, we should even tell you that you have been one of the greatest hearts of this new pulse of hope. To acknowledge this, I know it well, means to increase the weight of the burden that you have put on your back.

And now we will stop here a conversation that, maybe, will be necessary to take up again and continue at other times, on other topics, in other books. Let's stop here and help each other to make this collection together. Because there will need to be books—books that within our human limits attempt always to be in that *beyond* of which we have spoken—that is, to face now the questions that will be asked of us. This will not mean that we have already figured everything out, but that these questions pass through everything, and everyone welcomes and suffers them. Maybe we will be able to foresee the questions, not to snuff them out, but to bring them out, to clarify them in all their necessity even for ourselves.

In short, now another "work of our hands" begins. But isn't the Incarnation also this? To recognize our own limits and to create, within these limits, the instruments to walk together on the road that brings us to the future of the Father, which is the only possible future for man and his history, that future which is the meaning and the destiny of our birth?

LUIGI GIUSSANI
Biographical Note

Luigi Giovanni Giussani was born on October 15, 1922, in Desio, a small town in Brianza, north of Milan, Italy. His parents were Beniamino, an artist and a carpenter, and Angelina, who worked in a textile factory. He was a Socialist; she, a devout Catholic; and their role in the human and religious formation of young Giussani was fundamental.

Giussani entered the seminary of Venegono at the age of eleven and was ordained a priest on May 26, 1945. During high school, he fell in love with the study of literature, especially the works of the poet Giacomo Leopardi, because his "questions seemed to overshadow all others for me."

After his priestly ordination, his superiors decided the young Giussani should stay at the seminary to continue his studies and begin teaching. In 1954, he completed his doctorate in theology, with his thesis on *Man's Christian Sense According to Reinhold Niebuhr*. During that time, Giussani came to realize that underneath the apparent flourishing of Catholicism in Italy, a deep crisis was already brewing: the separation of faith from daily life, the contrast between tradition and current ways of thinking, and morality reduced to moralism. Though they knew the doctrines and dogmas, young people were deep down ignorant of the Church and were growing distant.

Seeing this, Giussani received permission from his superiors to teach religion in a public high school. Beginning in 1954, he taught at Liceo Berchet, a high school in Milan with a focus on the classics, where he remained until 1967. His presence in the school gave new energy to Gioventù Studentesca (GS or "Student Youth") and gave it the contours of a true movement. So began the history of Communion and Liberation.

Beginning with the 1964–65 school year, Fr. Giussani taught at the Catholic University of the Sacred Heart in Milan, a position that he would hold until 1990. An organic synthesis of what he taught was published in Italian between 1986 and 1992 in the form of the three-volume *PerCorso*, or "itinerary": *The Religious Sense, At the Origin of the Christian Claim*, and *Why the Church? The Religious Sense* has been translated into twenty-three languages.

In the early 1970s, Fr. Giussani became directly involved with a group of students at the Catholic University of Milan. Years of great dynamism, they saw the expansion of the movement into every realm of life: high school, university, in parishes, in factories, and in the workplace.

In 1977, he published *Il rischio educativo* (*The Risk of Education*), containing the fruit of his reflections on over twenty years of experience as an educator. It would become one of his most widely read and translated books.

The beginning of the 1990s brought the appearance of the first signs of the illness that would accompany him for over a decade, increasing in severity up until his death. It was also during these years that Giussani presented a number of his most enduring meditations to the movement: *Riconoscere Cristo* (*Recognizing Christ*), *Il Tempo e il Tempio* (*Time and the Temple*), and *È, Se Opera* (*He Is, if He Is At Work*).

During this period he also edited a series entitled *I libri dello spirito cristiano* (*Books of the Christian Spirit*) and provided the liner notes for a collection of classical music albums, *Spirto Gentil,* produced with Deutsche Grammophon. In 1995 he received the International Catholic Culture Prize in Bassano del Grappa.

On February 22, 2005, he died in his home in Milan. The funeral Mass was celebrated in the Duomo in Milan by then-Cardinal and Prefect of the Congregation for the Doctrine of the Faith, Joseph Ratzinger, serving as the personal representative of Pope St. John Paul II. He was buried in the Monumentale Cemetery in Milan. His tomb has become the destination for a steady stream of pilgrims from Italy and around the world.

At the end of the Mass celebrated at the Duomo in Milan on the seventh anniversary of Fr. Giussani's death, on February 22, 2012, Fr. Julian Carrón, Giussani's successor as leader of Communion and Liberation, announced that he had submitted the request to open the cause for canonization of the priest from Desio. The petition was accepted by Cardinal Angelo Scola, Archbishop of Milan.

GIOVANNI TESTORI

Biographical Note

Giovanni Testori was an Italian writer, journalist, poet, art and literary critic, playwright, screenwriter, theater director, and painter.

He was born in 1923, in Novate Milanese, a town on the outskirts of Milan, to Edoardo Testori and Lina Paracchi. Already at seventeen the young Testori was contributing articles on art criticism to university magazines. He soon became involved in the debate between realism and abstract art that engulfed the Italian art scene in that era.

By the end of the 1940s, Testori had also developed a passion for the theater. In 1948, his first drama, *Catherine of God*, was performed, and in 1950, at the Verdi Theater in Padua, *The Lombards*.

Starting in 1952, he became a student of art historian Roberto Longhi and published his celebrated writings on the art of Lombardy and Piemonte from the sixteenth through the eighteenth centuries. His first novel, *The God of Roserio*, came out in 1954: it takes place on the outskirts of Lombardy, a setting to which the writer would return many times. In 1958, he published a book on the frescoes of the Church of San Bernardino in Ivrea. That same year *The Bridge of Ghisolfa*, a collection of short stories, came out, the first part of the cycle *The Secrets of Milan*, followed by *The MacMahon Guild* (1959) and by his debut at the Piccolo Teatro of Milan: *Maria Brasca* (1960).

The 1960s were marked by his friendship with film director Luchino Visconti. In the summer of 1960, Visconti presented *Rocco and His Brothers* at the cinema exhibition in Venice, whose script was taken from stories in Testori's *The Bridge of Ghisolfa*. When in 1961 *L'Arialda*, the fourth installment of the *Secrets*, arrived at the Teatro Nuovo of Milan, directed by Visconti, the play was withdrawn and both men were accused of producing a text that—thanks to its compassionate depiction of homosexuality—was deemed "greatly offensive to the common feeling of modesty."

In 1965, *The Triumphs* came out: a monumental poem of almost 12,000 verses, with reference to the author's own love life, to the paintings of Géricault, and to the last trip of Saint Charles Borromeo to the Sacro Monte of Varallo. It was the first book of a poetic trilogy dedicated to his life companion, Alain Toubas, followed by *Love* (1968) and *Forever* (1970).

Testori returned to the theater in 1967 with *The Nun of Monza*. The play debuted again under the direction of Visconti at the Teatro Quirino of Rome. Testori explained his theatrical poetics in *The Womb of the Theater*, which appeared in the journal *Paragone* in 1968.

In 1972, Rizzoli published *L'Ambleto*, a re-writing of Shakespeare's tragedy, *Hamlet*. The text represents the incarnation of a language created by the author, a pastiche in which inflections in dialect live alongside terms derived from Spanish, French, Latin, and many neologisms.

Testori remained engaged with art criticism. In 1973, he was involved in the exhibition *The Seventeenth Century in Lombardy*. At the same time, through a series of showings in public and private galleries, Testori continued to promote the activity of young contemporary artists who had been neglected by critics.

On July 20, 1977, Testori's mother died; she had always been the most beloved family member in his life. The period of pain and recollection for her loss coincided with his return to the Christian faith, which he had never formally abandoned, but which he had always lived in the awareness and torment of the contradictions of life. In this context, his play *Conversations with Death* (1978) was born, performed in more than a hundred churches, theaters, and cultural centers all over Italy.

In the mid-1970s, Testori took over the position previously held by Pier Paolo Pasolini as commentator on the front page of *Corriere della Sera*. Many of his most significant pieces touched on current events. These reflections were collected by Testori, together with other articles that had come out in *Il Sabato*, in the volume *The Majesty of Life*, published by Rizzoli in 1982.

During this period, Testori drew close to the ecclesial movement Communion and Liberation, beginning a friendship with its founder, Father Luigi Giussani, with whom he would publish the dialogue *The Meaning of Birth* (1980).

It was through his relationship with the young people from the movement that *Interview with Mary* was born, a play that was staged in over 400 Italian churches. This became a trilogy, with *Factum Est* (1981) and *Post-Hamlet* (1983). *Factum Est* was written for Andrea Soffiantini and the newly-formed En Route Theater Company, founded by Testori together with Emanuele Banterle.

The year 1984 opened with the publication of *The Betrothed Put to the Test: A Theatrical Action in Two Days*. The main actors were Franco Parenti and Lucia Morlacchi; Andrée Ruth Shammah directed the play.

Testori continued to contribute essays and occasional writing to the world of Renaissance and contemporary art, while he also set forth his ideas of a theater concentrated solely on the word, starting work on the first *Brancia trilogy*—three plays written for the actor Franco Branciaroli: *Confiteor* (1985), *In Exitu* (1988), and *Verbò Autosacramental* (1989). The first production of *In Exitu* was held at the Teatro della Pergola in Florence, but for one evening it was performed at the foot of the grand staircase of the Central Station of Milan, where the play was set against the background of prostitution and drug addiction.

In 1990, Testori's health worsened and he was in and out of the San Raffaele hospital in Milan. He finished *Translation of the First Letter to Corinthians by Saint Paul* (1991) and produced a second "Brancia-trilogy": *Sfaust* (1990), *sdisOrè* (1991)—performed by Franco Branciaroli for the En Route Company, directed by Testori with the help of Banterle—and *The Three Laments,* published posthumously in 1994, a Dantean triptych.

The writer died at San Raffaele on March 16, 1993.

PUBLISHER'S NOTE

The Meaning of Birth presents a double challenge for an English-language publisher: it requires both careful translation and editing since the Italian text is derived from a transcript of a recorded conversation. While every effort has been made to maintain strict fidelity to the meaning of the original, some minor editing has been done to make the text more accessible for readers.

The publisher would like to extend profound thanks to the Associazione Giovanni Testori and the Fraternity of Communion and Liberation for their kind assistance. Thanks also must go to Rowan Williams for the foreword, Fr. José Medina for the original suggestion that this book ought to be available in English, Matthew Henry for his excellent translation, and Sandro Chierici and Laura Ferrario for their advice and support along the way.

This book was set in Adobe Caslon Pro, designed by
Carol Twombly and released in 1990. The typeface is
named after the British typefounder William Caslon
(1692–1766) and grew out of Twombly's study of Caslon's
specimen sheets. Though Caslon began his career making
"exotic" typefaces—Hebrew, Arabic, and Coptic—his
Roman typeface became the standard for text printed in
English for most of the eighteenth century, including the
Declaration of Independence.

This book was designed by Shannon Carter, Ian Creeger,
and Gregory Wolfe. It was published in hardcover,
paperback, and electronic formats by Slant Books,
Seattle, Washington.

The cover image is *Natività* by William Congdon (oil on
Masonite, 129 x 118 cm.). Collection: Ministero dello
Sviluppo Economico, Rome. © The William G. Congdon
Foundation, Milano, Italy. www.congdonfoundation.com

CPSIA information can be obtained
at www.ICGtesting.com
Printed in the USA
BVHW081058291121
622764BV00003B/315